The Culture for Quality:
Effective Faculty Teams
Edited by Patt VanDyke

Copyright © 1995 by Prescott Publishing Co.
106 S. Main St., Maryville, Mo. 64468
1-800-528-5197

Designed by Scott Pummell

Printed in the United States of America
First Printing: 1995
10 9 8 7 6 5 4 3 2 1

Library of Congress Cataloging in Publication Data
VanDyke, Patt.
    The culture for quality: effective faculty teams / Patt
VanDyke
    p. cm.
    ISBN 0-9633819-1-1

    1. School management and organization. 2. Quality control.
I. Title
LB2805.V36 1995   371.2
                                         QBI94-21204
ISBN 0-9633819-1-1: $24.95

PRESCOTT PUBLISHING

THE
CULTURE
FOR
QUALITY

Effective
Faculty
Teams

Edited By
Patt VanDyke

TABLE OF CONTENTS

THE
CULTURE
FOR
QUALITY

PREFACE
Patt VanDyke   v

**INTRODUCTION: DEVELOPING THE
CULTURE FOR QUALITY**
Annelle Weymuth   xiii

1 **KEY QUALITY INDICATORS**
Patt VanDyke   1

2 **TEAM COURSE PREPARATION**
*Richard C. Detmer, Linda Null,
Carol Spradling, Roger Von Holzen*   23

3 **DEVELOPING LIFE VALUES**
Janet K. Reusser, James A. Herauf   42

4 **BUILDING MULTIMEDIA PRESENTATIONS**
Patricia Lucido, Diane M. Krueger   68

5 **G**OAL **S**ETTING **W**ORKSHOPS
David C. Oehler   **84**

6 **T**EAM-**B**ASED **I**NSTRUCTIONAL **P**LANNING
Georgene A. Timko, Connie J. Ury   **103**

7 **T**EAMWORK AND **P**ROGRAM **D**EVELOPMENT
David Hancock, Patrick McLaughlin,
Roger Woods   **117**

8 **B**ENCHMARKING FOR **C**OURSE **I**MPROVEMENT
Harlan Higginbotham   **143**

Effective Faculty Teams

Preface

BY PATT VANDYKE

A book about functioning faculty teams in a regional university will surprise some who work in an academic setting. But skeptics—particularly those who mutter as they read—may soon be heard to grumble, "Why, we do *this* all the time. Well . . . something a lot like this at any rate."

What does the muttering skeptic mean by "this"? What has been identified as familiar in these accounts of teams doing academic work? What characteristics of selfless, directed group activity are most attractive to a vigorously self-reliant and independent faculty member?

Certain findings about group cohesion provide a starting

point from which to approach these questions. First of all, some say that the environment for higher education within the last decade has created a siege mentality within higher education. From this perspective, outside the gates of academe crowds of politicians, accreditors, regulators, and business leaders annually seize new battering rams for another rush on the fortress. The hollow reverberations of each successive hit—accountability! faculty work loads! student performances! performance funding!—have created a situation particularly conducive to the development of purposeful groups within colleges and universities. For the besieged faculty in this scenario, the apprehension about the threats from outside the university has prompted more cohesion within the university than is usual. However, others might note that the tension between gown and town is long-standing, occasionally murderous, and based on a division faculty liken to the one that Matthew Arnold saw as a constant struggle between the forces of sweetness and light and the Philistines. Those who take this longer view would be less likely to acknowledge current banging at the gate and stress that faculty generally, and often rightly, perceive threats to the ways they do things from outside the university. Regardless, the cohesion of academic teams, whether attributed to recent or historic causes, is likely based on the perception of threat from the outside.

A second situation enhancing group cohesion is a sense of shared failure. Facile causality would link this notion to the vulnerability of higher education noted above on the assumption that academics everywhere have accepted the resounding thumps on the gates and have ruefully gone about their work with a difference. A thoughtful look at the cases we present here points to a more sobering reason. Let us assume that Northwest Missouri State University is somewhat typical of regional, public universities, at the least. The average faculty member at our institution is directly involved with teaching, preparing to teach, evaluating, advising, and conducting the professional work of a teacher and scholar a minimum of 60 hours a week. Not one of the faculty I know feels he or she has "kept up with the field," particularly in this age when information expands with breathtaking rapidity. Even if much of that information is second-rate, the scholar-teacher will not know that it is until the materials have been examined. Top quality academic journals have two to three years' backlog, and new electronic journals spring up like dragon's teeth. The amount of information to be scanned is daunting. And, faculty all know that students have changed a great deal in the past few decades. The modern university teacher faces, on a daily basis, bright students who do not learn the way the teacher learned, who do not gain information from reading but from seeing and doing, and who have fairly immediate access to the same overwhelming amount of information that awaits the seasoned professional. Individuals in universities now find themselves thwarted by what there is still to learn about their subject area, their teaching methods, and their students.

The most common barrier to high performance on our campus is time, and I assume we are somewhat typical in this, too. Perhaps faculty may be working together better than before simply because our shared failure is that we cannot individually keep up, manage it all, juggle all the balls tossed to us. Consequently, a team effort focused on a project that will promote higher quality while reserving some precious time for the other activities of the scholar, teacher, and advisor has a good chance of powerful support. Shared failure does encourage solidarity and cohesion. Teams and the work of teams may be one of the best hopes for managing complexity.

Groups are more likely to be cohesive if the members themselves have certain characteristics. For example, if the members have similar personalities, attitudes, and social backgrounds, the likelihood of good group cohesion is increased. All of us tend to hire those that we think will fit into our work place, those who are already a lot like us or who show a willingness to become a lot like us. In addition, in higher education, the love of the discipline tends to level some other distinctions within a department. Further, in an institution with a strong teaching mission such as ours, many departments pride themselves on universally strong scores on student evaluations of their teaching and advising; this pride, oftentimes competitive, encourages cohesion and teamwork. Faculty feel an individual responsibility for contributing a strong course and well-prepared students to the department's program and to their colleagues. In a lean, highly prescriptive program, each course and each learning experience take on a heightened value, and those who teach courses "in the major" are very aware of the responsibility they have accepted for the group. Colleagues tell me that they are more careful to meet group expectations for a course than they would have been a decade ago, and they note that they spend a good deal of their time in departmental committee work aligning their work practically and philosophically with that of others. These factors are all highly significant ones for group cohesion and team building.

Group cohesion is also affected by other features typical of a small department. The physical proximity of a department's members aids in the development of cohesion and better teamwork. The similarity of what each member does in a department also leads to group cohesion. In the cases here, faculty teach the same courses, work with students at the same level, and interact with each other about common issues and common goals on a daily basis. Typically, faculty who have particular strengths in curriculum development, assessment, and student development gravitate toward those committees, providing continuity and experience to the group. The next logical step for these groups will be cross-functional teams, which will deal with broadly-based questions such as how training and orientation of new faculty affect advising and student success. This venture might comfortably begin with joint meetings of the whole committees if the committees are small, but will most likely begin with joint sub-committees, since this pattern of group problem-solving is familiar to the faculty. Joint sub-committees would have a distinct advantage in that the size could be kept smaller and other key factors of group cohesion could be considered.

Finally, group cohesion is enhanced by patient and systematic "out of the box" thinking activities oftentimes initiated by either the administration directly or by a key Faculty Senate committee addressing an administrative request. At their best, these activities help departments develop group goals and show them the processes by which to reach those goals. The campus has a sense of "connectedness," and the work of a small departmental team and the individuals on it is seen as a unique fleshing out of a college or university mission statement. The small team has internalized and personalized its work in terms of the larger group's goals. As a consequence, cohesion within the small group is enhanced as is its cohesion with the larger group. That cohesion is the foundation for cross-departmental teams, perhaps the next breakthrough for planning and improvement in higher education.

Those who work with group dynamics and group cohesion recognize that a group will begin to pull together and work on meaningful tasks when certain features are present in the individuals themselves, in the situations they face, or in the group itself. Certainly, administrators and faculty leaders should formulate work groups with an eye to group cohesiveness, taking care to address issues of proximity, function, personality, and status. But, all of those calculations will not mean much if the leadership is not able to help the group clarify reachable goals that make a vital connection between the work of the individuals, the work of the team, and the fundamental work of the university.

In the upcoming chapters, some of the faculty involved in team projects at Northwest will share their processes and their projects. These efforts will demonstrate the power of academic teams to address systematically and creatively problems that no one faculty member could manage so well alone. Briefly, several teams focused on a shared course or a program of study and used their collective efforts in order to make major improvements to a common responsibility. For example, a team in one college focused on weaknesses in a program, developed a rigorous plan to improve the program, and implemented its recommendations. The success of their efforts can be inferred from the recent competitive record of students graduating from the program and passing a national licensure examination. Another team concentrated its efforts on a common course all of the faculty had to teach and divided the work of preparing, delivering, and evaluating the course materials so that each member of the department is responsible for an identified component of the course. Naturally, they are proud of the efficiency of their joint effort, but they stress that the important thing is the quality of the effort. Each of them may concentrate on a particular facet of the course and develop the best materials or strategy for presentation possible, knowing that their colleagues are working on other components with the same diligence and professionalism. All the faculty responsible for teaching a general education CORE course aligned the rapid changes in their field with the University mission and went through a paradigm shift. The course they now teach supports a general education program stressing the lifetime learner, is better received by students, and is philosophically and pedagogically sounder.

Still other teams have sought to change the way they work

or to understand their common origins with colleagues. First of all, one team found that a change in the way their unit was managed encouraged them to initiate exemplary service programming. The programming they began has taken on a life of its own and accounts for an increasing number of contacts between the service and the students and faculty of Northwest each year. Two teams formed around a common problem— involving students in larger lecture sections in active learning. One of the two teams' members shared ideas and resources, sought joint professional development grants, and laid the groundwork to change instruction in several departments within the same college. The other built on the work of benchmarking partners to dramatically increase student learning. Finally, a team of faculty explored the common purposes they felt must exist between the courses they taught. In the process of their discussions, they recognized not only the bonds between them, which they fully articulated, but they acknowledged that more should be done to celebrate and expand their common purposes. They continue to meet as a planning team to develop a new, interdisciplinary course.

Whether the teams have met to address a known and shared experience or to identify precisely the experiences that they believe they may share, the results have been rewarding personally and institutionally. Of course, it is our intention that others reading these chapters will recognize the collective force of an academic team empowered to change its processes and its programs to achieve something better than it had before. From our experience, we believe that potent academic teams form in an environment that encourages and expects excellence. At Northwest, we have kept our eyes on what we call "a culture of quality" for a long time. Achieving such a culture has been a driving force in our planning and development activities for nearly a decade. We believe that such an environment provides the impetus for change, the support for risk-taking, the commitment to continuous improvement. This culture is the culture for quality.

Patt VanDyke

TEAMWORK

Q DEVELOPING THE CULTURE FOR QUALITY

Annelle Weymuth

An Introduction to the Development of the "Culture of Quality"

⫻ As an assessment template, the Baldrige asked the critical questions any institution needs to ask, whether industrial or educational. How do we help raise quality performance practices and expectations. ⫻

from p. xv

Through the late 1980s and the beginning of the 1990s, Northwest Missouri State University has grown into one of the nation's most respected and forward looking state universities.

But it wasn't easy. Real change rarely occurs on a campus of higher education. However, Northwest's legacy of excellence in education, coupled with the futuristic vision of an electronic campus, have helped create a change in campus culture.

The myth of a rural Missouri state-supported school as a tranquil, undisturbed, simplistic university is being challenged by beliefs in the importance of technology, exposure to diversity, but most of all the expectation of a high quality learning experience.

Northwest developed its values and sense of education early in the beginning of this century. In 1905, Northwest was born by legislative action and housed 212 students in a rather impromptu setting in Maryville, Missouri. Growing from a storefront that was converted to classrooms, the campus matured first as the Fifth District Normal School, then as State Teachers College and State College. Finally in 1971, Northwest earned the status of State University and now boasts a population of over 6,000. As the school matured, the campus itself also grew. It took nearly four years to construct the administration building, but the school was finally then able to move out of the humble storefront and into more comfortable surroundings.

Nothing has come easily to this region, but the people reflected a stick-to-it attitude, worked hard, and were willing to be persistent for the establishment of higher education in the northwest portion of the state.

With firmly rooted values from early in this century, Northwest prepared itself for the upcoming century by adapting its campus to two revolutionary aspects on the educational horizon. Northwest met the technological age head first with an integrated, campus-wide computing system and also began revamping   the university through a comprehensive, quality-based philosophy.

"The Electronic Campus," unique in the nation, began in 1987 to offer every Northwest student, faculty member and

An Introduction

ber and staff employee access to the computing network of more than 2,400 terminals. The services include voice-video-data connections with each residence hall room and faculty office.

Even before implementing the Electronic Campus, Northwest demonstrated its aggressive vision of education through a program that has proven just as revolutionary as the computing system. The university adopted a series of programs that provided a means of analysis, evaluation and planning in order to strengthen the undergraduate education and campus life environments.

In the fall of 1984, newly-appointed President Dean L. Hubbard appointed a twenty-five member Masterplan Steering Committee with advice from the Faculty Senate. Charged with overseeing the development of a strategic quality masterplan for the university, the committee published its first planning document, "Building the Foundations."

Three broad considerations influenced the development of the masterplan. First, it should result in both strategic and comprehensive planning. Secondly, the committee agreed that it should include a large segment of the university community in the process, and finally it should provide for continual updating of the five-year plan. In order to ensure that planning would be strategic, the committee then moved to identify thirty-seven "environmental assumptions" and selected five "mega-trends" as critical factors in planning for the future viability of the university.

The first part of the plan was an internal and external strategic audit. The internal audit involved reviewing trends within the institution, previous planning documents, accreditation reports, plus attitudinal surveys which sought to quantify the needs, expectations, and level of satisfaction of the key groups such as students, faculty, and alumni. The external audit consisted of reviewing the Missouri Coordinating Board for Higher Education's (CBHE) mandates, as well as other mandates from the state and national levels.

The next phase of the planning process involved the refinement of a mission statement. Previous efforts at mission refinement dating back to the early seventies were embedded in the final statement of mission. The Faculty Senate, Student Senate, and Board of Regents all voted acceptance of the mission statement.

Over 120 members of the university community participated in the planning effort. Twelve committees developed goals which represented a natural extension of the mission statement and were integrated with the planning assumptions. The mission, environmental assumptions and megatrends provided a context for twelve subcommittees which developed short- and long-term goals for curriculum and instruction, campus life, community/regional services, development and alumni affairs, finance, personnel, institutional governance, general support services, learning resources, environmental quality, student affairs, and faculty affairs.

Ongoing development of specific action plans were coupled with the goals. In order to expedite this critical phase of the process, assignments were made to various departments on campus which developed objectives and action steps needed in guiding the university efforts during the school year. This process was repeated on an annual basis so that each year an action plan could be approved reflecting the mission and goals of the institution. The action plans were integrated into a comprehensive document which provides a framework for budget development. Then the final phase was evaluation of the progress in achieving the goals and updating the planning assumptions, revising goals, and updating of the planning assumptions, adjusting goals and objectives as necessary.

In the fall of 1986, the university's masterplan was again updated, this time with a sharper focus on improving the quality of undergraduate education. Seven categories of activity were considered crucial to improving quality: admissions, placement and learning support; general education/liberal arts; the living/learning environment; and general institutional policies/governance. More than 200 ideas were cataloged. Four decision drivers were adopted: 1) a "talent development" (i.e., value-added) definition of academic quality; 2) a commitment to the proposition that access and rigor are not incompatible; 3) the belief that strategies to improve quality must reflect and incorporate high expectations, involvement, assessment and feedback; and 4) the conviction that time-on-task is an important consideration when improving educational quality. In the context of these decision drivers, forty-two of the 200 recommendations were adopted as goals. In order to accomplish these goals, forty specific action steps were adopted to be accomplished on a seven-year time line. The resulting plan was called "The Culture of Quality Plan for the Improvement of Undergraduate Education," or simply, "The Culture of Quality."

The transition from a culture that focused on education for the sake of securing a position once the student graduated, to one that focused on education as a quality endeavor as well as preparing for a career was a very slow process both for the student and the faculty. As the campus was accomplishing their masterplan, one would have witnessed much more emphasis on committee accomplishments with an eye on the mission, goal, or action steps associated with the directive. One would have also found a change in the student's attitudes from a predominately rural perspective to a more global, cosmopolitan perspective.

The Culture of Quality over the years was quiet but powerful. A different sense of pride was emerging from both faculty and students as we began receiving national attention for our Electronic Campus. Every residence hall room and faculty office was equipped with a computer terminal on line with word processing and spreadsheet capabilities from a VAX system, as well as capabilities of e-mail, library access, and registration for classes, to mention a few. More students benefited from work with a faculty mentor as undergraduate research slowly shifted from service areas to instruction. Using contract services such as Service Master and ARA resulted in savings for the institution. The use of wood chips for boilers also showed significant savings on fossil fuel use.

By fall 1991, it was clear that the original Culture of Quality plan was going to be accomplished ahead of schedule. Thus, the fall planning retreat was devoted to the study of the Malcolm Baldrige National Quality Award criteria for possible incorporation into the University's planning process. As an assessment template, the Baldrige asked the critical questions any institution needs to ask, whether industrial or educational. How do we help raise quality performance practices and expectations? The Baldrige serves as a working tool for planning, training, and assessment.

At the beginning of the 1992-93 academic year, a new steering committee was appointed. One of the tasks accomplished was a pilot-test of the Baldrige Criteria. Seven sub-committees were established, one for each of the seven Baldrige Categories: leadership, information and analysis, strategic quality planning, human resource development and management, management of process quality, quality and operational results, and customer focus and satisfaction. The number of members on each sub-committee reflected the number of examination items subsumed under that category. For example, leadership had three members while human resource management had five, and so forth. Some sub-committees, however, had more than the minimum number since student members were paired with faculty. Each sub-committee member (or pair) was assigned one item to study, understand, and apply. Sub-committees were free to select any area or department within the University as a pilot-test site. The end result was that every sub-committee at the end of six weeks endorsed their category and its examination items for inclusion in Northwest's planning process.

The pilot committee examining the Baldrige became known as the Culture of Quality Review Committee. The composition of the committee was very position-specific, e.g. president of Faculty Senate, chair of Budget and Planning of Faculty Senate, delegate from Council on Teacher Education. Because of this yearly change in committee composition, an orientation to the Baldrige needed to occur. The retraining of new people was frustrating in some ways, especially to those administrators retaining membership on the committee, but it enabled the learning process to disseminate throughout the campus each year to new faculty and student leaders. The forty people representing all parts of the university are continuing to focus on the Baldrige as an assessment model to give direction to our planning for the nineties. Northwest was one of the first universities to apply for the Missouri Quality Award in the area of education, in May of 1994. A site visit was granted in September of 1994. The campus saw this as a wonderful validation of all the efforts of those on campus who have dedicated time and energy to the task of getting us to the point where we could be selected for a site visit. The feedback from those evaluating us using the Missouri criteria which is almost identical to the Baldrige criteria will be useful for planning and improvement. Whether we win an award is not the issue. The culture has changed and a higher level of quality can be evidenced in all areas of the University from classroom instruction to the care of the grounds. The plans that will be derived from the Missouri Quality Award assessment process will take Northwest Missouri State University successfully into the next century.

Effective Faculty Teams   xix

ANNELLE WEYMUTH

Annelle Weymuth is the Executive Assistant to the President at Northwest Missouri State University in Maryville, Missouri. She has a B.S. in vocational home economics from Purdue University, an M.S. in family studies from Indiana University, and is currently completing her Ph.D. from the University of Missouri at Columbia in human development and family studies with a collateral area of higher education administration.

Weymuth came to Northwest in 1976 to teach family courses in the Home Economics Department. She served as president of the state Home Economics Association from 1987-89, is a certified family life educator, member of the scholastic honorary Kappa Omicron Nu, and past president of American Association of University Women, Maryville Branch, and Wesley Foundation.

Weymuth is also Northwest's Equal Opportunity Officer and Americans with Disability Act Coordinator. She is one of the category chairpersons on the Culture of Quality Steering Committee and has served on numerous committees in the area of faculty governance.

An Introduction

TEAMWORK

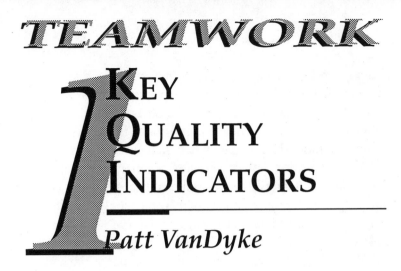

KEY QUALITY INDICATORS

Patt VanDyke

The Degree of Fit Between Academic Programs and Customers

// Working from the broad outlines of the Culture of Quality Planning Model, each department has started with its core values and its assumptions about the essential skills and knowledge that must be internalized by students graduating from the program. //

from p. 19

Northwest began thinking about key quality indicators long before it called them that. In early, cabinet-level discussions about quality and the pursuit of quality, frustrated participants spent some time trying to translate the term to other practices more comfortable for those in higher education, such as behavioral objectives and long-term goals.

Frankly, in retrospect, the participants shared a disquieting perception that these indicators were part of business as usual, an old truth dressed out in trendier clothes that we would all wear awkwardly at first but be comfortable in later. Seasoned cabinet members had seen widely hailed initiatives in the past trucked out as though they were new when they were not. On campuses, such innovations are labeled flavors-of-the-month and are glared and grumped to death by the faculty. We did not realize the latent power in the initial pursuit of what we came to know—unit by unit—as our key quality indicators.

When we first began to work with the concept, we had not clearly defined our terms. Our midwestern work ethic and our academic bent for individual contributions had led us to believe that if we each did our work correctly, we collectively would offer quality to our students. Departments hired good faculty; the university provided a dynamic and technologically sophisticated work place, supported the library and performing arts activities, and funded projects that were targeted on improvements. All of us made it our practice to respond positively to substantive changes recommended by accrediting groups. We had not thought of asking our students, alumni, and employers what they were looking for in our graduates, our majors, our campus environment, and our services.

As the Cabinet has now defined the phrase and as Northwest is working with it at present, a key quality indicator means an important hallmark or demonstration of quality from the customer's perspective. In other words, it is quality in the words of the customer.

Let me pause briefly here to address the "customer" idea. In an academic environment, particularly in areas over which the faculty has primary authority and responsibility, we found it very helpful to brainstorm a rather lengthy list of the constituents/patrons/customers of the service or program and of the institution as a whole. From the outset, all levels of the institution agreed that students are the primary customers of instruction but not the primary constituency shaping the curriculum. Since we had implemented a rather comprehensive assessment system using multiple measures of assessment to address a broad range of accountability issues, we had experience gathering information from graduate school contacts, from employers, and from alumni. These constituencies we saw as more credible customers of the curriculum than currently enrolled students.

In addition, we had been through several accreditation visits which had given us very valuable feedback from external consultants, whose work and experiences helped shape key programs in the institution. For example, recognized by the state as Northwest's areas of excellence are agriculture, business, and education. Agriculture had one of its programs—Agriculture Education—evaluated by a rigorous Department of Elementary and Secondary Education review team as exemplary, a rating given to very, very few programs. In addition, the College of Business quite recently completed a comprehensive self-study for accreditation and renewed its formal accreditation by the Assembly of Collegiate Business Schools and Programs (ACBSP). The College of Education passed the DESE review and led the campus in a meticulous three year program to prepare for a comprehensive NCATE review. In other words, in every one of our designated areas of excellence, we have been fortunate to align our quality journey with the critiques of stakeholders, customers, and consultants and to reflect their suggestions in our planning and implementation.

For departmental faculty, then, the key quality indicators have provided an internally developed set of targets based on significant input from key customer groups and external consultants. The processes of developing the lists and of validating the current indicators have reinforced values and relationships from which departments may have drifted in the preceding decade when so many different interest groups were challenging higher education and demanding accountability.

Fundamentally, when a department writes its key quality indicators in consultation with its major constituents and validates them, it becomes very focused on what it is about. Assessment becomes more relevant; curriculum discussions take place in a new light; classroom assignments become richer, more flexible. Faculty assign more team projects to classes and establish a different context for presentations and written work.

In the remainder of this chapter, I would like to discuss in detail the work in Owens Library with the key quality indicators, so that the reader gets a picture of how the process worked and what value it holds for academic support units on college campuses. Then I would like to overview the process and the results in selected departments, one from each of the four colleges at Northwest, so that the broader possibilities of application and benefits can be seen. This mixture of the specific and the general should provide a starting place for anyone interested in the lessons learned and possible implementation strategies.

The development of the Owens Library Key Quality Indicators took place, as they say, very slowly over a long period of time and then suddenly all at once. Meeting in early January of 1993 with a feedback group of faculty, students, and staff, an Owens team led a brainstorming session which generated a two-column list of customer expectations for service, ambiance, coverage, and policies. The team then identified common themes on the list by using an affinity diagram, clustering all the items under two rubrics—Collections and Service. At that point, the process stalled, quite likely for two reasons. First, in their zeal to reduce the long list of items to something manageable, the team had gone too far and had grouped internal operational processes with direct public contact processes. Second, the Owens team had not concentrated on the concept of the key quality indicator as quality in the customer's words. In the fall of 1994 the new director jump-started the project by interviewing fifty percent of the staff, seeking their key quality indicators for a library. Using this list of indicators and the original list generated by the patrons, the director refocused the discussion, and, within two days, distributed a consensus list of nine key quality indicators, tied to the three broad areas of Collections, Internal Operations, and Service and Atmosphere (fig. 1).

In the case of Owens Library, the key quality indicators proved immediately useful for the staff to use in defining its expectations for two suppliers: a company that binds books, theses, and periodicals; and a photocopy repair business that has a maintenance contract with Northwest. Very early on, the director made it clear to the staff that we should link what our patrons demanded of us in quality service to a failure to produce high quality service and products by a supplier. We could say to the supplier that a service had to be more accurate or more timely because inaccuracy or lateness kept us from achieving our high standards. Without those high standards, we could not meet and exceed the expectations of our patrons. Suddenly, we were not asking for ourselves, but we were champions for the patrons who expected specific behaviors from us. We were asking for those very important people.

Key quality indicators have sharpened other parts of our operation as well. Since we are a state institution, we must follow the state bidding process. Part of that process would seem to have us turn over our needs to the lowest bidder were it not for the joint imperative that the bid also reflect the best. The assurance of supplier quality lies in the accuracy with

OWENS LIBRARY KEY QUALITY INDICATORS

Components to Address	Key Quality Indicators	Quality Descriptors	Quality in Patron's Words	Methods of Evaluation
Collections	Accessibility	Ease of use, Location, Open for use	Can find and use	Mystery shoppers, surveys, audits, formal evaluation of the collection, cross-functional analyses
	Currency	Materials, Technology	Modern and up-to-date	
	Scope	Materials, Alternative materials, Alternative resources	Good coverage	Benchmarking, audits
Internal Operations	Accuracy	Procedures, Responses	Works smoothly and purposefully	Surveys, audits, I.L.L. logs
	Timeliness	Processes, Information	Gets work done promptly	Audits, logs, surveys Cross-functional process evaluation
Service and Atmosphere	Helpful, Friendly	Supportive and pro-active, Pleasant and approachable, Responsive, Inviting	Cares about helping me	Mystery shoppers, listening posts, comment cards, logs, surveys
	Informed	Knows the collection and strategies, Knows the technology, Knows policies		
	Professional	Focused on patron's needs and wants, Orderly, logical		

Fig. 1

which a unit can operationalize its key quality indicators as specifications and can keep accurate quality records of the supplier's work and products as they relate to the specifications driven by the key quality indicators. For the Owens staff—long frustrated with shoddy workmanship, inconsistent turn around time, and slow response time—the key quality indicators provide a clear framework in which they will develop more exact specifications for critical bidding processes. They will more carefully define "best" by linking the key quality indicators to the supplier services and will find themselves less often riding with the low bid supplier in the driver's seat. The key quality indicators have shown them a way to handle an external process that they had not handled proactively before.

The next step for the Owens Library will be to set standard performances for each of the operations and processes that support the achievement of a key quality indicator. For example, when a new book comes into Owens, it is not accessible to the patron until and unless several vital steps are completed. These steps range from accurate cataloging through entering the information onto our On-line Public Access Catalog (OPAC, an electronic catalog) to shelving the book correctly so it can be identified and located by the patron. It is not truly accessible to those who do not know the book is now in the collection unless the faculty liaisons in Owens contact targeted potential users of the book. Each of the teams accountable for these operations will have to set the performance standards that it needs to meet and improve work processes to meet those standards. In order to provide a framework for continuous quality improvement in these linked operations, the director had a staff member, Pat Danner, the acquisitions specialist, use the work of Myron Tribus to prepare a discussion document for Owens faculty and staff. That document was intended to help the Owens faculty and staff understand the significance of high and clear work performance standards for each component of the library as that component's work related to a key quality indicator.

Improving Processes Improves Patron Satisfaction
Key Quality Indicator—Accessibility

Question: If every function or person in Owens Library does the job ninety-five percent right and on time . . .

Owens Subject Librarians, after consulting with Northwest faculty, select the materials	.95
Collections team plans the selection process	.95
Acquisitions places the order	.95
Supplier delivers the material	.95
Acquisitions certifies the material meets our specifications and is acceptable	.95
Library Use Instruction team trains patrons	.95
Computing Support keeps OPAC running	.95
Cataloging places the material on OPAC	.95

Patron finds book on OPAC   .95

Circulation checks out the book
to the patron   .95

Reference assists patron in
finding related material and
supplemental information   .95

Owens Subject Librarians,
Northwest faculty, and Library
Administration promote the library
and tell interested patrons the
book is in   .95

...what is the likelihood of getting useful and appropriate materials to the patron on time?

Answer: $(.95)^{12} = 54$ percent of the time

In two weeks the director followed this discussion paper with a "what if" document, which used the same basic framework recalculated with some modest improvements factored in. The staff and faculty informally discussed the stretch goals each unit would have to set to address the key quality indicator of accessibility. That discussion will be formalized beginning in the spring semester.

The project has also led to requests for specific assistance. One unit, Technical Services, initiated a request for more training in how to measure and track accuracy and how to establish indicators that would show trends that were tied directly to the key quality indicators. The team leader of Distribution and the director are each working her way through professional studies of library evaluation methodologies to identify techniques that will measure the Owens Library's achievement of key quality indicators, using best practices in the field. It will be a logical step to benchmark superior processes when we can more exactly measure what it is we are doing.

The academic departments at Northwest were well ahead of Owens Library in the initial stages, since they were following a seven-step planning model developed by the president of the university, his cabinet, and the four academic deans. This model was influenced by work done with the Baldrige criteria over the past three years. From its inception, this initiative placed the specifics of the project in the hands of the faculty. It avoided prescription, setting performance standards, and imposing time-lines for the entire process, albeit consensus had been reached with the deans and chairs about a time-line for the first two steps of the process. The strength of this process was that faculty teams knew immediately that they were in charge of discovering and working with the key quality indicators for their disciplines and their constituencies.

The Culture of Quality Planning Process is a sequenced process that will lead to clarification of goals and purposes, coherence in curricular and instructional development, heightened correspondence between assessment and key quality indicators, management by fact, and continuous quality improvement. The steps are:

1. Identify Key Quality Indicators.
2. Validate them with the customer.
3. Develop a strategy to accomplish them.
4. Formulate an assessment strategy to track performance.
5. Establish base-line data and track trends.
6. Identify superior processes when weaknesses are identified (e.g. benchmark other organizations or institutions.)
7. Set stretch goals.

Northwest's Foundation Board has provided new monies to support this process and will provide funds to departments or units that successfully make their way through these steps. In addition, the president has assigned the director of the Talent Development Center to assist the departments at each step of the process. Other resources on campus—such as the training in quality techniques and theory available to us through our Institute of Quality Productivity—will be tapped at appropriate times. Currently, nearly twenty faculty and administration members are attending a quality practices class taught by the president of the university and the dean of the College of Business, Computer Science, and Government. Northwest has exponentially increased the pool of trainers and mentors within the last year and a half with our training and learning activities. Consequently, the departments find themselves in an environment where continuous improvement has become the standard, but they also find themselves actively, not nominally, in charge of the changes that matter most to them. In this environment and with these issues, the departments function as "committees of the whole." This academic phrase means that the entire department works as one committee with a common purpose, intensity, and focus. In academia, many department meetings are marred by internecine squabbles, old wars over commas and formats: those meetings advance little and settle less. But when a department says that the department met as a committee of the whole, one knows that the group has formed a team and has functioned purposefully and harmoniously on that occasion.

In 1994, Northwest's four colleges were the College of Arts and Humanities; the College of Business, Government, and Computer Science; the College of Science and Agriculture; and the College of Education. All of the departments have completed the first two stages of the Culture of Quality Planning Process at the minimum. Many are well beyond that.

Several are down the list, notably to step five, because of other projects, such as Missouri's required comprehensive assessment mandate. But, some of the departments at step five will probably prefer now to back up and come down the list again. With their key quality indicators in place, they may wish to revisit their choices for their major field examinations; they may wish to develop a local assessment package that more clearly responds to the key quality indicators, for example. Some early benchmarking activity may be viewed as premature if the department did not have the key quality indicators in mind. The benchmark partner might be revisited or other contacts made with new partners who work with the same sort of constituencies. But so far, we have found that good work and good plans have been directed, almost intuitively, toward the features that matter. Oftentimes, the revisions that we are facing now are of alignment rather than total invention.

One of the departments I would like to showcase is from the College of Arts and Humanities. The Department of Art, chaired by Mr. Lee Hageman, has become a campus leader in responding to quality initiatives. The process adopted in this department reflects the basic work style of its members. First of all, the chairman gave the group a springboard into the process by sharing information developed in the Department of Human Environmental Science (HES). HES had made Northwest's initial foray into working with advisory boards to establish and validate key quality indicators. Each member of the department privately considered the indicators and the process developed by HES before coming up with his or her own list. These lists were shared at a department meeting geared toward identifying the common themes and principles held by members of the department. As with other of their quality initiatives and conversations, the task became an opportunity to share personal values and create an even stronger community within the department.

The department developed a common list, which was a sampler of the department's work. This sampler was taken by the faculty individually to selected advanced classes. Students in those classes were asked to reflect on the ideas and to privately write down their key quality indicators. Later, the faculty set aside some time in the respective courses to discuss and refine the ideas students had about the qualities that a graduate leaving the program in art should have. In an attempt to consider elements that it might have missed, the department also sought input from other departments and chairs. For example, they asked them to read their key quality indicators as a check on the richness and inclusiveness of the indicators that were being confirmed through the process. Finally, the department created a comprehensive set of possible indicators to send to selected alumni who had graduated within the last five years. This group was asked to validate and comment on the indicators they saw, indicators that by now reflected the work of individuals whose ideas had been tempered and honed through discussion, reflection, comparison, and evaluation.

The response from the alumni truly overwhelmed the department. The return rate was high, something which is always satisfying to a department. But the nature of the responses was what made the experience memorable. It was clear that the graduates cared very much about the quality of the education they had received and had spent a good deal of time thinking about the separate items. Some had prioritized the list, some had highlighted key attributes, some had rephrased and revised ideas and made them fresher and more powerful. Some had written notes and clarifications and letters; the passion of the alumni about the quality of the education they had received touched the faculty and reaffirmed the power and importance of their work.

One of the departments in the College of Agriculture and

Science is the Department of Agriculture, chaired by Dr. Arley Larson. Their process in establishing their indicators is also instructive. The members of the department met shortly before one of the regularly scheduled meetings with their advisory board to brainstorm answers to the question "What characteristics should our graduates have?" The department easily came up with a list. At the advisory board meeting, the employers and agricultural experts who attended were asked to respond to the same question from their point of view: As customers, what characteristics did they expect to find in Northwest's agriculture graduates? The advisory board brainstormed its list, which, to the delight of the members of the department, corresponded very well with the list generated by the department. In effect, this effort with the advisory board confirmed the work of the department with the employers and alumni on the advisory board, since the two lists overlapped. In the next phase of the process, the dean of the college received written feedback on the same topic from the members of the required senior seminar class. Their written lists corresponded in the main to the lists generated by the faculty and by the advisory board. The department feels that the overlap of the lists by the two key customer groups constitutes a type of validation and has moved to the next stages of the Culture of Quality planning model.

The curriculum in agriculture has been examined from the point of view of the key quality indicators. One of the key quality indicators was "skilled in communication." The department traced both writing and speaking tasks that are required in specific classes in each of the programs available to the major, to assure itself that the course requirements were advancing the key quality indicators. The same principle guided their evaluation of "skilled in computing," since several courses require work with specific applications that are standard in the field. Finally, the department is considering the role of assessment and seeking more sophisticated ways to assess the key quality indicators on which they and their chief customer groups are in total agreement. As a team, they are moving systematically through the steps of the Culture of Quality Planning Process.

The Department of Marketing and Management in the College of Business, Government, and Computer Science, chaired by Dr. Ed Ballantyne, consistently functions as a team. Beginning in 1991, the department began a series of informal TQM meetings and mini-retreats focused on continuously improving the work of the department, the quality of the graduates, and the effectiveness of the curriculum. At one of the early fall meetings in 1991, the team identified common concerns that it wished to address: abilities in students graduating from the program and characteristics in the system that produced such graduates. As the department explored the idea of abilities in the students graduating, they generated a list that contained skills, knowledge in the field, and experiences, but the consensus was that the department could immediately focus on writing and communication skills. They collectively acknowledged that they were going to be learning about what they wanted to accomplish while they were trying to do it. Everyone agreed to take the risk.

Indeed, the initial efforts were flawed. First of all, the team had agreed to a general goal: all courses would have more writing and speaking. However, they had not specified a sequence of writing tasks to avoid putting students through the same types of assignments with the same learning/writing outcomes over and over. Instead, members of the department zealously added writing, speaking, listening, and presenting assignments to their classes. In a short time, faculty were staggering under the load of constant review of written work, and students were planning on cutting back their schedules to handle the increased expectations in all courses for written work. The increased cycle times for both evaluation and graduation were serious concerns.

In the fall of 1993, the department met during our traditional walk-out day, the Friday before Homecoming. At that daylong meeting, the department established base-line information about who was doing what and began working more systematically toward fundamental outcomes. They decided to concentrate certain skills and tasks in different levels of the program and to sequence the student's experiences in learning more systematically. For example, a required course, Managerial Communication, had formerly been taken by juniors and seniors and had included the development of the professional resume. The course was refocused so that it became, in effect, a communications intensive prerequisite to other courses in the department. In this course, students are given team and individual experiences in writing, speaking, listening, and presenting—all skills demanded in the courses that will follow. By advisement, the course is scheduled in the first semester of the sophomore year. The chairman of the department keeps the enrollment in the course at twenty-five students, which parallels the same number of students in most English composition classes. The course is meant to establish the foundation skills that the other courses will build on, so that students move to more sophisticated communication tasks sequentially with the faculty members indicating higher expectations for performance at each level of course work. All of these decisions and initiatives have been team decisions initiated and led by the department's curriculum committee.

The department has a relatively complex system of validation of the key quality indicators it has developed. Since 1991, the chair has been using a matrix to track feedback from regional employers to monitor the effectiveness of graduates from the program. In addition, the chair uses a university advisory board, the Industrial Advisory Board, to review the currency of the department's key quality indicators and has surveyed as many as 250 employers nationwide gathering feedback about course topics.

Most recently the department has completed an initial survey of institutions statewide to determine the nature and effectiveness of advising systems as a prelude to a benchmarking activity, which it views as just another tool in its continuous quality improvement journey.

As anticipated, a mature department with significant involvement in TQM or CQI, or one with a stronger assessment background, could realistically have some of its activities at a fairly advanced stage of the Culture of Quality Planning Process and other activities at a more rudimentary level. This department does find itself in that situation and seems clearly focused on addressing baseline information needs and continuously refining what it has done based on more systematic feedback from alumni. They are confident, however, that they are managing the change paradigm and clearly focusing on systematic Continuous Quality Improvement through empowered team responses to key quality indicators.

The final case to round out our examples from the four colleges at Northwest is the Department of Educational Administration, chaired by Dr. Max Ruhl, in the College of Education. This department was selected because it is a department that has developed strong partnerships with its students, who become alumni and employers at graduation. This department teaches graduate classes directed to experienced teachers who are taking advanced work to assume principalships and superintendencies, so the relationship they have with their customers over time is a complex one.

Northwest has aligned its practices and all written and illustrative material with the new accreditation standards of the National Council for Accreditation of Teacher Education (NCATE). This cycle of self-study has positioned the departments in the College of Education to move naturally from a clear articulation of the knowledge base to statements of exit level competencies graduates of the program would have. In the case of the Department of Educational Administration, the faculty consulted the Department of Elementary and Secondary Education at the state level and the Principal's Assessment Center before drafting a list of 155 outcomes that operationalized the knowledge base and the nine competencies suggested by the department. The department went to its advisory board of principals and superintendents with the list for feedback and validation. They summarized all the information and reduced the original list of outcomes slightly. The nine competencies remained unchanged, since all groups were in agreement with those.

As part of the next phase of the project, the department added courses and rigorously incorporated oral communication activities throughout the curriculum. Each of the outcomes was assigned to a specific course. In addition, the department specified for that outcome whether it was to be reviewed or presented in depth, whether it was to be a major component of that particular course or a supporting component.

At this stage, the faculty teams looked at the comprehensive examinations that concluded the programs and aligned those with the competencies identified and with the outcomes. The examinations became criterion-referenced and flowed naturally from the philosophy and practices of the department. This latter activity, which the department had dreaded attempting, turned out to be one of their most powerful team efforts, bringing them together to solve a problem that capped all the preceding work.

This work had been accomplished when the entire campus began working on key quality indicators, but the department recognized that, even though there was some overlap, not all of the nine competencies were observable or directly measurable. In addition, the department affirmed the value of the competencies in telling them what they were to teach, but they also acknowledged the worth of key quality indicators in directing them toward measurable hallmarks of quality. Currently, they have identified eight key quality indicators to be used in tandem with the nine competencies. The two lists will provide what the chairman calls "a bridge between theory and practice." The department has already begun thinking about the quality and type of assessment appropriate to such outcomes-focused programming and is utilizing its advisory board and students to develop more powerful "in baskets"— scenarios calling for reflective thinking, good communication, and well-grounded decisions.

As we have seen, each unit has adapted the project according to the work styles, philosophic orientations, and current practices of the department so that the problem from definition to implementation has been its to solve. Working from the broad outlines of the Culture of Quality planning model, each department has started with its core values and its assumptions about the essential skills and knowledge that must be internalized by students graduating from the program. Each, too, has either forged new alliances with constituencies or has found ways to strengthen the bonds between the department and its students and alumni as well as with those who employ graduates from our programs. Some have been able to use the project or components of it to encourage shared thinking and teamwork, developing a stronger academic unit. Others have renewed their commitment to teamwork through this project because of its substantial impact on the curriculum and courses. In retrospect, I think all would attest to the applicability of the following entry in the *Diary of Anais Nin, Volume III* : "There are very few human beings who receive the truth, complete and staggering, by instant illumination. Most of them acquire it fragment by fragment, on a small scale, by successive developments, cellularly, like a laborious mosaic." Stepping back from this mosaic, we delight in the play of color, the form and the substance of what we have made together in our key quality indicators project.

REFERENCES

Nin, Anais. *The Diary of Anais Nin, Volume III: 1939-1944*. New York: Harcourt Brace Jovanovich.

PATT VANDYKE

P att VanDyke holds both a master of arts degree and a doctorate from the University of Wisconsin—Madison. Specializing in twentieth century British and American literature, she taught in the Department of English at Northwest Missouri State University for eighteen years before accepting her first administrative assignment, developing a comprehensive academic support center and initiating Northwest's assessment program. Other administrative assignments followed, including a semester as interim director of Owens Library where she is implementing the Baldrige criteria in a self-directed work team environment.

Professionally, she has authored and presented papers about tendentiousness in the American short story, particularly in the writings of women and minorities. She has published poetry and given poetry readings as well as delivered occasional papers on aspects in the writings of contemporary American authors. In the last five years, she has helped Northwest offer two highly regarded conferences on quality, editing a book called *Keeping the Promise* after the first conference. This work captured some of the seminal efforts toward quality in undergraduate education.

TEAMWORK

2 TEAM COURSE PREPARATION

Richard C. Detmer
Linda Null
Carol Spradling
Roger Von Holzen

"...the teamwork effort put forth by the instructors of CS130 helps make it a very successful course, both in the eyes of the instructors and of the students enrolled. "

from p. 37

CAMPUS SETTING

In the fall of 1987, Northwest Missouri State University inaugurated its ambitious Electronic Campus project to accelerate learning opportunities for students and enrich faculty teaching and research. The Electronic Campus, the first of its kind on a public college or university campus, provides a central cluster of VAX computers, a terminal in each residence hall room and faculty or staff office, and groups of terminals in the library and classroom buildings. Through this mainframe system, students have access to the library catalog, electronic mail, a word processing system, an encyclopedia, Internet, scheduling of video segments on the campus cable channel, and much, much more.

Northwest also has several microcomputer laboratories. Two of these are in classrooms used primarily for teaching Using Computers, the required computer literacy course. These were stand-alone systems until Ethernet cards were added and Digital Equipment's Pathworks networking software was installed. In 1991 these computers were replaced by 80386DX-based systems (fifteen in each room) which are still in service. Each of these machines has four MB of main memory, a 40 MB hard drive, a 3 1/2-inch floppy drive and a 5 1/4-inch floppy drive. This gives sufficient power for most Microsoft Windows applications, particularly because the bulk of the files can be stored on the network server. This combination of mainframe and microcomputer systems, networked together, provides tremendous flexibility and power.

The Using Computers course is designed to familiarize students with the benefits and drawbacks of both large and small computer systems. Because most students take this course during their freshman year, it serves as the primary introduction to campus computing. Approximately one-third of the course is spent doing mainframe applications, including WPS, the word processing system that is accessible to students in their residence hall rooms. The remainder of the laboratory work is devoted to microcomputer applications, primarily Microsoft Works for Windows.

COURSE HISTORY

Originally, the only introductory computing courses taught at Northwest were programming courses, as was the case for most universities and colleges in the seventies and eighties. However, the need for a course more oriented toward computer literacy was soon very evident, and Using Computers (CS130) was created. In 1984, a handful of instructors began teaching the two credit-hour course. One instructor was designated as the course coordinator, overseeing approximately twelve sections per semester. It was the coordinator's job to ensure that hardware was functioning correctly, all software was available and working, and laboratory workbooks were updated and made available to students. There was little coordination done in regards to the lecture and examination materials.

The course was divided up into lectures and laboratories; lecturing was done in one room with one instructor, and laboratories were taught in a different room by a different instructor. The lectures covered concepts such as computer operation, computer hardware, computer ethics, history of computing, computer languages, computer crime, and various terms and definitions associated with computers. The goal of the lectures was to familiarize students with computers and their impact on society.

The laboratory component of the course gave students hands-on experience with various software packages. On laboratory days, students would meet in the computer laboratory and work on Apple IIe microcomputers. Software packages included Introduction to a PC, Logo, word processing (Bank Street Writer), spreadsheet (Multi-Plan), logic concepts (Rocky's Boots), and various educational software programs. Laboratory workbooks, created by the instructors teaching the course, were provided to each student. These workbooks included any handouts the students might need and practice exercises.

The dichotomous nature of the lecture and laboratory components of the course resulted from the presentation of the material in two forums. Therefore, a decision was made to create classrooms where lectures and laboratories could be integrated. In 1987, two classrooms were designated as CS130 teaching and laboratory rooms. At this time, all hardware was switched to IBM compatibles, which required new software as well. Originally, eighteen 8088-based machines with dual 5 1/4-inch floppy disk drives were used in each of these rooms. This was also a good time for the department to rethink the course structure and objectives as well. The new three credit-hour CS130 course was changed to keep up with advances in computer technology and education.

For its first six years, CS130 was offered as a required course for mathematics and business majors and an elective for other university students, many of whom took the course because they were interested in learning about computers and how to use them. In 1990, CS130 was selected as a core general studies course. Instead of offering twelve sections per semester, the department more than doubled the offerings, resulting in approximately twenty-five sections per semester. Significantly more effort was required to coordinate the class and keep track of hardware and software. Regular group meetings were established for CS130 instructors to help them communicate any software suggestions, problems, teaching innovations and various announcements regarding CS130. These meetings were scheduled during a free time period and proved to be a very useful resource for anyone involved with teaching the course.

Even with twenty-five sections per semester, instructors were not sharing the bulk of materials necessary for the course. Each instructor wrote examinations to cover lecture material and to test laboratory skills, homework assignments, and laboratory exercises. Some sharing was being done, though, in the laboratory workbook, which contained not only instructions to students, but also a small pool of possible assignments instructors could choose from if they desired.

A small core of instructors slowly evolved into a group that worked together to develop materials, removing a significant amount of redundancy and allowing each instructor more free time to modify and improve the materials being used. In 1989, a Culture of Quality university grant was awarded to support the development of course materials. This group of three faculty members shared assignments, lecture notes, lecture examinations, laboratory examinations, and handout materials for the students. Much of the handout material was added to the laboratory workbook, which was being modified every semester.

The team approach used by this small group of instructors was very successful. Other instructors grouped together and created another team, functioning in much the same way as the first team. As instructors continued to witness the benefits of the team approach, more of them joined one of the teams. In the fall of 1992, a single team was established and all of the instructors began to work together.

Present Course

The current Using Computers is primarily a hands-on course which emphasizes learning by doing, although there is some lecturing. Students spend most of their class time working in pairs at computers, learning a variety of software products including word processing, spreadsheets and database packages, as well as putting into practice what they have read about in the textbook and heard in lecture. Students in the course have a textbook that they are required to read. For the more technical material, the textbook is supplemented by class lectures.

The hands-on component is conducted by the regular course instructor, with a laboratory assistant available to help with students' questions. Students gain experience with both microcomputers and the campus network. They have tutorials that they work through at their own pace, as part of the hands-on component of the course. Within the class, students also work on assignments, practice laboratory examinations, and design and implement a project, which integrates several applications.

Student requirements for the Using Computers course are: quizzes, assignments, an individual project, laboratory examinations, written examinations, and a final examination. These requirements involve the Using Computers instructors in intensive preparation of materials, although the preparation of these materials does vary from semester to semester depending on events, such as a new textbook or new software.

The preparation of materials for the Using Computers course has been broken into the following course-related tasks:

Course Syllabus Preparation: A detailed course syllabus is prepared, outlining when reading and lecture material will be covered, when quizzes will be given, when assignments and the individual project are due, and when laboratory examinations and written examinations will be given. A student version of the syllabus is prepared which details these requirements on a weekly basis. An instructor version of the syllabus, which details these requirements on a daily basis, is also prepared. The daily syllabus also includes information such as what materials should be brought to class for which lecture, reminders to announce to students, and listings of chapter readings and assignments.

Scheduling for the course addresses conflicts, such as

equipment, materials, varying lengths of classroom meetings (sections of the course meet two and a half hours each week, either seventy-five minutes per day twice a week, or fifty minutes per day three times a week), and the loss of class periods due to university and calendar-related vacation days.

Laboratory Workbook: Students use a laboratory workbook which contains assignments and supplementary materials such as lecture notes, copies of transparencies, and review questions. This workbook must be edited each semester and updated to incorporate course revisions resulting from software and/or textbook changes and modifications of assignments and notes. This task includes considerations such as consistent format, order of materials in the laboratory workbook, and details as to what material is on the back of a page the students will be removing to hand in.

Quizzes: Six quizzes, each typically covering two textbook chapters, are given throughout the semester. The quizzes are designed to test the students' knowledge of the reading and lecture materials. The format for each quiz consists of ten matching questions covering terminology used in the course. Two versions of each quiz are prepared. Both versions of the quiz contain the same questions, but the questions are scrambled in order to discourage dishonesty. The quizzes are given in all classes during a one week period with the understanding that they may not be returned to the students during that week.

Assignments: The eleven assignments cover a variety of computer software ranging from Electronic Campus information programs to specific software applications such as word processing, spreadsheets and database management. The preparation for each student assignment involves the development of precise directions for the students and the preparation of accompanying files, when appropriate.

Individual Project: Each student, near the end of the semester, designs an integrated application potentially useful in her or his future career. Project examples and specific directions for the student requirements are carefully chosen for this project. Students generally produce projects that combine uses of word processing, databases, spreadsheets, and graphics.

Laboratory Examinations: Three laboratory examinations are given to test students' mastery of various software applications. Four different versions of each laboratory examination and the accompanying files used in each examination are prepared. This task also includes the preparation of a sample laboratory examination which students use to review the required objectives. Due to the physical limitation of fifteen microcomputers in a class of thirty students, laboratory examinations are taken individually by students and are administered during two separate time periods. Half of the students take their laboratory examinations during one time period, while the other half of the students take their examinations during another. Laboratory examinations are scheduled during a one-week period and instructors may not return examinations to students during this week.

Written Examinations: Three written examinations are prepared to test the students' knowledge of the reading and lecture material and software. Relevant true/false and multiple choice questions are carefully selected to cover the course objectives and ensure that questions represent an appropriate distribution as reflected by the course materials. Two different versions of the examination are prepared with questions arranged in a different order. The different versions are intended to eliminate potential student copying. The written examination is given to all students during a common time scheduled in the evening. A common make-up examination time is scheduled at the beginning of the next week.

Final Examination: The comprehensive final examination incorporates questions from all class materials covered. A common time is scheduled for all students during final examination week.

Course instructors are divided each semester into teams of three instructors and assigned to one or more course-related task work groups. Each team consists of one team member who is given the responsibility of developing the material, a second team member who is responsible for the first proofreading of the material, and a third team member who is responsible for the final proofreading of the material. While the preparation of laboratory examinations and written examinations is intensive, the proofreading of these examinations is also time-consuming. For example, an instructor assigned to proofread a laboratory examination must "take" each version of the examination. This process can consume up to four hours. An instructor assigned to the primary proofreading of the written examination must verify that each question is clearly stated in the reading material, lecture notes or software. Often the primary proofreading responsibilities of the examinations may be just as difficult as the preparation. An effort is made to utilize known strengths of an instructor when assigning work group tasks. For example, instructors known to be good proofreaders are assigned more proofreading than writing, while instructors known for their ability to write test questions may be assigned the task of developing an examination. An effort is also made to fairly apportion assignments, i.e., team member assignments are correlated with the number of sections taught; a person teaching three sections has about three times as many duties as a person teaching a single section.

CS130 MEETINGS

At the heart of the effort to establish a workable team approach to teaching a computer literacy class are regularly scheduled meetings of the instructors. Each semester a specific time is set aside in the teaching schedule of all CS130 instructors for an hour long meeting.

The meetings are called by the CS130 coordinator, who generally sets the agenda. The meetings are typically held on a weekly basis during the fall semester due to the presence of new CS130 instructors and the introduction of new materials and/or revisions to the course. The focus of the meetings normally centers on scheduling problems, software-related questions, and discussions about examinations, quizzes and new materials being introduced. Demonstration of new software and discussion about possible future changes to the course are also frequent components of the CS130 meetings.

An important aspect of the meetings is aiding instructors who are teaching Using Computers for the first time. Veteran CS130 teachers often act in the role of mentors by assisting unseasoned instructors with lecture notes, software instruction and other routine aspects of the course. The goal of such mentoring efforts is to help maintain a consistent approach across all sections and instructors of the course.

Between CS130 meetings the coordinator sustains contact with the course instructors through electronic mail. E-mail messages are often used to inform instructors when they may return quizzes and examinations, to answer questions about software problems and/or solutions that may suddenly come up, and to announce any changes in the scheduled CS130 meetings.

During the spring semester, fewer meetings are normally held. This is primarily due to the fact that most or all of the CS130 instructors are veterans and that little new material is introduced during this time. E-mail therefore becomes the mainstay for coordinating the course and communicating with the instructors. The need for CS130 meetings is usually reduced to a monthly basis.

Summer school finds the CS130 instructors more on their own. If two instructors are teaching during the same session, though, they typically coordinate their course schedules and jointly construct quizzes, laboratory examinations and written examinations. Typically, a compressed version of the spring schedule is used as the summer course outline.

Overall, the goal of the CS130 meetings is to maintain the highest quality of instruction across all sections of the course. By meeting and communicating on a regular basis in such an open forum, the wisdom and knowledge of the varied instructors of the course is more readily brought forth and exchanged.

INSTRUCTOR INDEPENDENCE

It might appear that the team approach requires all instructors to teach the same material in the same way. However, quite the opposite is true. Instructors are encouraged to maintain individuality, and this is supported by the fact that teachers now have time to investigate and integrate new methods and ideas into the classroom. Writing examinations, homework assignments, and quizzes once demanded much of the instructors' time, but that time is now freed up by team contributions of these materials. Many instructors have developed additional materials for the classroom that, without the team approach, would not have been possible.

Instructors are encouraged to use a similar time frame in covering material so that examinations, quizzes, and assignments can be shared. But this in no way requires that individual instructors be in lock-step with each other. Some instructors lecture a great deal, while others lecture only a small percentage of the time. Some show videos to encourage class discussion and others do not. One instructor may choose to cover the topics from the lecture material in a slightly different order, use a different homework assignment, or give different or additional handouts than another instructor. These individual choices are supported and encouraged by the team approach to teaching CS130.

CS130 Teamwork—Conclusion

The team approach to teaching CS130 has a few disadvantages along with its many advantages. Meeting on a weekly basis during the fall semester, when most instructors are usually quite busy, prompts one complaint often heard among the team participants, which is that it requires too much time. Other negative comments about teaching CS130 that periodically surface mostly have to do with the course schedule. In devising a general course schedule that accommodates the varying lengths of the classroom meetings and accounts for school calendar-related disruptions (vacations), the instructors of the course find that there is limited flexibility in their teaching of the course. The schedule has set times for quizzes, laboratory examinations and textbook examinations. Therefore each instructor must maintain a close adherence to the course schedule. Returning graded quizzes and examinations to the students is also typically impeded by the need to make sure all sections have completed the quizzes and examinations.

Another disadvantage is found in laboratory and written examinations and quizzes. Because the writing of quizzes and examinations is often assigned to other instructors, some of the questions and problems that make it through the review process may not be those of choice for a particular instructor. An instructor is always given the opportunity to make his or her own version of the quiz or examination. Such an effort, though, is typically not undertaken due to time constraints.

Finally, one other criticism of teaching the course as a team effort is the large amount of material or specific topics that are included in the course schedule. The tight semester schedule most instructors function under is a result of the effort to accommodate the varying instructors' desires as to the material and topics presented in the course.

Although there are some drawbacks, the advantages far outweigh the disadvantages. During the fall and spring semesters, anywhere from twenty-two to twenty-seven sections of CS130 may be offered. Such a large number of sections results in the need for an ample collection of instructors, typically from eight to twelve. With most instructors usually teaching two or three sections, a tremendous amount of redundant effort would have to be undertaken by each instructor to devise the necessary course materials, if there were no effort to approach the course in a teamwork fashion. One of the most frequent arguments given in favor of continuing the CS130 team approach is the amount of time saved by the individual instructors over the course of a semester. Instead of writing all the quizzes and examinations for the course, each instructor normally writes only one or two quizzes and/or examinations. The effort in generating the needed course materials is thus spread evenly across all of the instructors.

With this joint effort to fabricate necessary course components comes the shared responsibility to ensure that the materials produced are of the highest quality. All materials are reviewed twice by other instructors before final duplication and distribution, an undertaking that few instructors have the time to do when they function independently. This effort helps to minimize the problems that often appear in course materials and examinations and thus leads to higher quality materials being presented to the students.

A third argument in favor of the team approach in teaching CS130 is the ease with which new instructors can be integrated. With common schedules and shared materials, new instructors find they can spend more time getting comfortable with the course material and writing their daily lessons.

The increased open time that most CS130 instructors experience due to the team approach enables them to devote more time to developing new materials for the course. This important side effect of the teamwork approach to teaching Using Computers strongly influences the pace at which the course evolves to reflect the current state of computer technology.

When a course such as CS130 has so many instructors, it is not uncommon for students, over time, to begin to express preferences for specific instructors through their enrollment patterns. It has been found, however, that the enrollment patterns with CS130 do not seem to reflect student preferences for specific instructors, but rather their preference for specific time slots. This minimization of student preferences may be the result of the consistency of instruction achieved across the many sections of CS130 and the coordinated teamwork undertaken.

A final argument for teamwork—consistency of instruction across the domain of CS130 classes—is evidenced by the data collected during the spring 1994 semester and supplied in the following chart. The mean percentage scores for the two sections reporting the highest and lowest class averages on the four examinations are listed. In each case, the differences in the means were not statistically significant at the 0.05 level.

	EXAMINATION NUMBER			
	1	**2**	**3**	**4**
Highest Mean	76.5	73.7	74.3	73.7
Lowest Mean	71.7	70.5	68.3	67.6

Team Course Preparation

In summation, the opposing arguments listed above show that the teamwork effort put forth by the instructors of CS130 helps make it a very successful course, both in the eyes of the instructors and of the students enrolled. The present approach to the preparation of these student materials has been an evolving process and by no means is complete in its development. The overall goals, though, of saving instructors preparation time and achieving the highest quality of instruction have clearly been accomplished using the team approach to teaching Using Computers.

RICHARD C. DETMER

Richard C. Detmer is a professor in Northwest Missouri State University's Computer Science and Information Systems Department. He had prior teaching experience at East Texas State University, Western Kentucky University, and the University of Tennessee at Chattanooga. He earned a doctorate in Mathematics from the University of Wisconsin and a bachelor of science in Mathematics from the University of Kentucky.

At Northwest, Detmer teaches a variety of computer science courses, ranging from computer literacy to theoretical senior-graduate courses and graduate courses designed for educators. He manages the local area network that serves the computer literacy classrooms, and frequently acts as an informal consultant on microcomputer problems. He is an active participant in his department's development of active learning environments. He is the author of an assembly language textbook and has a variety of presentations and published papers to his credit. He enjoys participating in professional computing organizations at local, regional, and national levels.

LINDA M. NULL

Linda M. Null is an assistant professor at Northwest Missouri Sate University in the Computer Science and Information Systems Department. Null began teaching computer science courses at Northwest in 1983, having received her bachelor of science in Mathematics and English Education, master of science in Mathematics Education, and master of science in School Computer Studies, all from Northwest. Before teaching computer science at Northwest, Null taught mathematics for two years in a Missouri public school, leaving high school teaching to accept a job in the mathematics department at Northwest and later teaching mathematics and computer science at a private Missouri college. In 1986 she was granted an educational leave and attended Iowa State University, where she earned a master of science in Computer Science in 1989, and a Ph.D. in Computer Science in 1991.

At Northwest, she is very involved with computer science research, course and curriculum development, faculty governance, and undergraduate research. Her research interests include the societal impact of computer technology and object-oriented database querying, concurrency control and security.

CAROL L. SPRADLING

Carol L. Spradling is an instructor at Northwest Missouri State University in the Computer Science and Information Systems Department. Spradling graduated with a bachelor of science in Accounting from Buena Vista College in Iowa, and received a master of science in School Computer Studies from Northwest Missouri State University.

Spradling worked for two years in public accounting and seven years in hospital accounting and finance at University of Iowa Hospitals and Clinics in Iowa City, Iowa. She is a registered non-practicing certified public accountant with the state of Iowa.

For the past six years she has been teaching at Northwest Missouri State University. At Northwest, she serves as a co-coordinator for the multisection Using Computers course and teaches Using Computers and Introduction to Pascal.

ROGER L. VON HOLZEN

Roger L. Von Holzen is an assistant professor at Northwest Missouri State University in the Computer Science and Information Systems Department. A 1977 graduate of the University of Wisconsin—Stevens Point with a bachelor of science in History and Broad Field Social Science, Von Holzen taught on the high school level for ten years. He began teaching at Northwest in 1987 after completing his master of science in Computer Education at Northwest. From 1990 to 1993, while on educational leave, Von Holzen completed his doctorate in Instructional Technology at Texas Tech University. Since returning to Northwest, he has been involved in the incorporation of presentation and multimedia tools into the classroom environment and with the continuous development of the department's general education computer literacy course.

TEAMWORK

3 DEVELOPING LIFE VALUES

Janet K. Reusser
James A. Herauf

❝ **The task forces serve as a vehicle and means to develop ownership within the overall large faculty team. When faculty members are divided into smaller task forces, the responsibility is more concentrated.** *❞*

from p. 56

Since the 1960s advancements in sophisticated diagnostic equipment and instruments have occured rapidly and impressively. Information relating to exercise, fitness, and health, substantiated with data based results, emerged the past thirty years and has infiltrated all aspects of society (Astrand, 29-31). It has been a ground- breaking and innovative time for health and physical education. Part of the innovation has occurred in the articulation of concepts and the development of new thrusts. Some of the subdisciplines that have emerged are wellness, preventive medicine, behavioral sciences (behavior change strategies), and cardiac rehabilitation. With the movement in society towards prevention, the concept of wellness has developed as an integral part of the discipline.

The development of the Health Objectives for the year 1990 and the subsequent Healthy People 2000 have given a significant impetus to the wellness movement. Healthy People 2000 has placed physical activity and fitness as the number one health objective for Americans.

Health and Wellness Distinction

To better understand the direction of the wellness and health movement it is important to make a distinction between these two terms. Health is the human condition with respect to social, physical, emotional, and mental dimensions. Each of these dimensions is characterized on a continuum of positive and negative endpoints (Bouchard et al.). The positive pole is associated with a capacity to enjoy life and to undertake the challenges of life and is the ultimate goal for individuals and society.

Wellness, on the other hand, is both a holistic concept and approach which accentuates a positive state of health in the individual considering biological and psychological well-being (Bouchard et al.). Wellness is not a static condition; rather, it is a movement toward a more positive state of health.

The wellness model can be applied to different aspects of an individual's life. Figure 1 shows the role physical activity plays in work and leisure and how it affects an individual's fitness level which then can affect health and wellness.

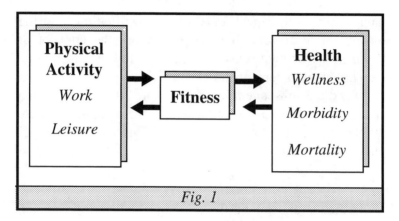

Fig. 1: A Schematic Concept of the Relationship Between Physical Activity, Fitness and Health (Bouchard et al.).

ROLE OF WELLNESS TO ACCOMMODATE DIVERSE SOCIETAL NEEDS

Both rising health care costs and the movement toward preventive medicine, education and rehabilitation services exacerbate the pressing need to address a daunting array of concerns (Shepard): 1) alcohol, 2) tobacco and drug use, 3) chronic diseases (cancer, chronic obstructive pulmonary diseases, cardiovascular considerations), 4) nutrition, 5) stress management, 6) mental health (balanced living), 7) sexually transmitted diseases, 8) human sexuality, 9) consumerism, 10) communicable diseases, and 11) overall physical fitness. Because of the scope of the concerns, the American population needs to look squarely at the health issues and approach health and wellness from a comprehensive viewpoint, which includes physical, mental, emotional, and social health. Only such an approach could hope to address the goal of living more effectively and improving the quality of life.

The overall intent and purpose of the general education life values and physical fitness core classes is to address the issues that confront all American citizens including the college-aged student. By designing an educational setting to "equip" students with skills and tools, it is anticipated that students are better able to make effective decisions regarding the central issues of health and wellness in our society: nutrition, sexuality, alcohol and other drugs, exercise habits, stress management, communicable diseases, cancer and cardiovascular risk reduction techniques. Through the courses, students develop competencies and grasp an in-depth understanding of physiology and anatomy and how the body responds to environmental factors and behavioral decisions. Since the campus population is indeed a reflection of society, by giving students the wellness experience they will become informed consumers, equipped with practical knowledge, tools and skills. They will develop a positive self-concept and self-esteem in preparation for their roles as contributing members of society.

TEAM WORK TO DEVELOP CORE COURSES SHARED VISION, CONSENSUS BUILDING, OWNERSHIP, SHARED DECISION MAKING

The development of the general education core courses emerged from a collaborative team effort. Northwest's administrators and faculty members, realizing that society was in need of health and wellness education, requested a complete review of the university's total general education program. The Department of Health, Physical Education, Recreation, and Dance (HPERD) faculty team considered not only the mission of the health and physical education department, but also the university mission. The university mission states the "university strives to provide a quality living-learning environment which will equip the individual for responsible participation in a rapidly changing society. This involves the common quest of educated people everywhere: the search for truth, an appreciation for physical well-being, and an active participation in the improvement of the human experience."

HPERD is committed to providing a quality environment which encourages the university community to be active, understand and maintain or improve emotional, physical, and intellectual well-being. The department's key quality indicators advocate that students will be able to: 1) effectively coordinate learning, 2) experience dignity, 3) realize self-worth, 4) accept responsibility, 5) face challenges, and 6) make wise decisions for the future.

The faculty team effort began with a shared vision and aligned university and department missions among faculty members. As the faculty reviewed social needs and trends and the direction of the profession and other institutions within the state and nation, the proposal of a four-hour life values and physical fitness requirement was developed. Faculty members at the outset agreed to share vision, develop ownership, exhibit shared decision making, and build consensus. Within the department and the university, as the new course proposal started taking form, it was obvious that specific training for faculty was critical. With insightful vision and the review of past success and failure of other health and physical education required courses, the team set the stage to incorporate existing institution instructional goals into the four hour requirement. The instructional goals that were decided upon were: use of science, practical skill application, reasoning about values, and self-directed lifelong learning. These carefully selected instructional goals and the incorporation of them into the courses gave the courses definition, direction, and continuity. With the central and specific focal point in place, the faculty are centered on the overall course description and objective (fig. 2).

Fig. 2

DEVELOPMENT OF THE LIFE VALUES AND PHYSICAL FITNESS WELLNESS MODEL

Team Emphasis

Consensus Building
Shared Decision Making
Ownership
Training

Institution Instructional Goals

Science
Practical Skills
Self-Directed Life-Long Learning
Reasoning About Values

Fig. 2: The focal point is the university and department mission combined with a shared vision by administrators and faculty team members.

INSTITUTION INSTRUCTIONAL GOALS MET THROUGH LIFE VALUES AND PHYSICAL FITNESS

Science

Health education is interdisciplinary in nature. Content material is derived from sociology, psychology, medicine, economics, biology, chemistry, and physical education. Because of this, students are exposed to and are expected to be able to work with methods of scientific inquiry and to understand that process. In addition to the emphasis on providing students with scientifically accurate information, the courses examine health problems and issues from the standpoint of how they have influenced society politically, socially and economically. An example would be how technological advancements in dealing with heart disease have affected health care in our society. Students are expected to be able to analyze health matters using a scientific approach so as to be able to make effective decisions on health matters during the course of their lifetimes.

Practical Skills and Reasoning About Values

Health and wellness instruction examines a variety of viewpoints on issues that affect individuals and society with an emphasis on application. First of all, because it is part of our shared vision, opportunities are presented for students to develop practical skills for application to their lives. Students learn to examine and clarify their own values and to understand how the maintenance and/or improvement of their individual health affects society as a whole. This enables students to look at health and wellness as a lifelong process. By studying the varied topics, students are able to develop a better understanding of the values that other people hold, which leads to more effective interaction with others in our society.

The team agreed that health and wellness education are both content and process. Consequently, they designed the educational experience to reflect both. These two components make it possible to prepare students to evaluate information, clarify values, develop decision-making skills, and determine alternative behaviors for living effectively and improving the quality of life.

Capability of Self-Directed Learning

Health and wellness education provides students with the lifelong ability for expansion and application of knowledge and skills gained in the educational process by making them informed members of a dialogue about their own well being. Students acquire practical knowledge and decision-making skills that will lead to a lifetime commitment to a healthy lifestyle, thereby enhancing their ability to enjoy life and meet their own interests and needs. The process of health and wellness education will help students set personal lifetime goals that are satisfying and useful, will lead to a reduced need for health care later in life, and reduce the risk of premature illness and death.

As a consequence, wellness-driven physical eduction parallels health care and instruction in the larger society. Health care and instruction have moved from a treatment orientation to prevention and conservation. Conservation of well being implies having knowledge and skills to avoid high risk behaviors, so that quality of life is increased as well as longevity.

To effectively develop the courses incorporating such goals as conservation of well being, the faculty met frequently to develop the life values and physical fitness requirement proposal for presentation to the faculty curriculum committee and faculty senate. Several faculty team members presented evidence for a wellness model adoption. Teaching life values and physical fitness to stimulate self-directed, responsible, lifelong learners became the overall thrust and emphasis for the curricular change. With the approval from the faculty curriculum committee, faculty senate, and Board of Regents, the foundation for the life value and physical fitness courses and wellness was conceptualized.

With administrative approval the cornerstones were laid for an exciting directional change for the health and physical education general education requirement. The faculty team worked diligently to put the plan on paper into action. It was now time to put the foundation under the castle in the air. Specific course syllabi, course objectives, textbook adoption, student competencies, performance indicators, grading scale, selection and assignment of faculty, and overall class scheduling were the tasks at hand. By 1989 the new configuration for the core requirement was established, approved, and implemented (fig. 3).

THE FOUR-HOUR CORE

The four-hour core is divided into three specific areas:
• a two-hour lifetime wellness lecture class which includes nutrition; sexually transmitted diseases; communicable disease; physical fitness; cancer; stress and stress management; mental health; human sexuality; alcohol, tobacco and other drugs; health consumerism; and cardiovascular diseases;
• a one-hour physical fitness assessment course (Lifetime Wellness Laboratory). This course gives students a physical fitness "report card." Students are assessed on health related components including muscular strength and endurance, cardiovascular endurance, body composition (percent body fat), flexibility, and blood pressure.
• a final one-hour credit class is an exposure to activities selected from a series of courses. These one-hour activity courses include lifelong aerobic carry over activities, such as

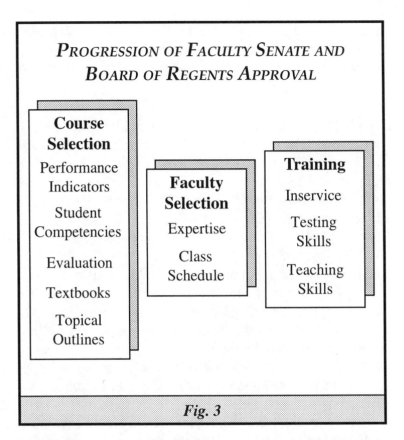

PROGRESSION OF FACULTY SENATE AND BOARD OF REGENTS APPROVAL

Course Selection
Performance Indicators
Student Competencies
Evaluation
Textbooks
Topical Outlines

Faculty Selection
Expertise
Class Schedule

Training
Inservice
Testing Skills
Teaching Skills

Fig. 3

Fig. 3: Progression of Faculty Senate and Board of Regents Approval for the life values and physical fitnes wellness curriculum.

volleyball; jogging; weight training and conditioning; racquetball; casting and angling; tennis; golf; badminton; aerobic, jazz and social dance; and swimming. Also included is an individualized fitness program (water exercise, super circuit, and aerobic walking). Students with medical and physical limitations and disabilities enroll in an individualized restricted activity course. Disabled students, under the direction of an expert faculty member in disabilities, develop their personalized fitness and wellness program based upon their specific strengths, needs, and limitations.

FACULTY TEAM DEVELOPMENT

The dissemination of facts and information is not enough in the education arena today. The use of practical and hands-on experience for students facilitates the learning process. To reiterate, the institution instructional goals are the focal point for the life value and wellness model. One of the most crucial dimensions of the teamwork is faculty development. Several dynamics—shared vision, consensus building, shared decision making, and ownership—have already been identified in the process of the adoption of the life values wellness model.

With the diversity and large number of faculty who teach within the wellness curriculum and involvement of other departments in the core, there was a need for specialized training for the faculty themselves to gain competencies in different areas. Training became a dominant factor in the development of faculty as effective communicators and instructors.

Coordinators for each area of the courses Lifetime Wellness lecture, Lifetime Wellness Laboratory or fitness assessment, and activity courses are assigned by the department chair. These coordinators work in collaboration with the department chair, the Campus Health Service and the Chemical Abuse Resource Education program to effectively perform and achieve the university and department missions. The coordinators are given the latitude to develop faculty through different avenues. The coordinators are responsible for all aspects of assessment, conducting inservice sessions, circulating pertinent, relevant, and newly founded research and current research to the faculty.

STRATEGIES TO DEVELOP SHARED VISION, CONSENSUS BUILDING, SHARED DECISION MAKING, OWNERSHIP, AND TRAINING

Inservice Sessions: The primary vehicles to develop the important aspects of teamwork—shared vision, consensus building, shared decision making, ownership and training skills—has been through inservice meetings, regularly scheduled meetings and long range planning and faculty development workshops. These periodic sessions allow for faculty members to have a voice and to share their ideas, thoughts, personal vision, suggestions, and concerns regarding the direction of the classes. Typically, inservice meetings are held two or three times a year. However, whenever a pressing issue or opportunity arises more meetings or sessions are held. Prior to the inservice the coordinator circulates an agenda which includes specific issues and items for discussion and review. Coordinators allow faculty to give input and feedback regarding the courses and faculty members develop a sense of empowerment and responsibility. Faculty suggestions are discussed during the inservice meetings. The open format of the inservice settings fosters non-restrictive dialogue among the faculty team.

Throughout the semester, the coordinator visits regularly with faculty to facilitate the flow of information and keep all faculty involved and instructors posted on pertinent course information and administrative decisions. Frequent memorandums are circulated to faculty, department chair and the athletic director to keep the lines of communication open. Without communication there is a loss of continuity and teaching standardization; professional isolation can result. A major purpose of this approach is to ensure a true commonality for the core courses.

Consensus Building and
Shared Decision Making

Continual Communication: Throughout the term, the Lifetime Wellness lecture, Lifetime Wellness Laboratory, and activity course faculty are asked to contribute their thoughts, support and opinions for the revision of exams, exam formats, and course syllabus. The coordinator visits regularly with faculty to facilitate the flow of information and keep all faculty involved and posted regarding pertinent course information and administrative decisions.

With continual communication between coordinators and administrators, faculty are involved with numerous activities that encourage and enhance consensus building. The open discussion allows for faculty to share their ideas and share the decision-making responsibilities. Issues vary with the specific needs for each course to move forward. For example, since the Lifetime Wellness lab (fitness assessment) uses a standard lab manual written by Northwest faculty, it is possible to review and revise the manual when the need arises. Currently, the lab manual is in the review stage. A volunteer (task force) of faculty are currently revising the lab manual— upgrading, expanding, and developing specific areas, specifically exercise and fitness for the disabled. Editorial input and format suggestions from all lab instructors will be solicited and considered before the final draft will be submitted to the publishing company. Lifetime Wellness lecture faculty are assigned to topic areas to provide information for other faculty.

Long Range Planning and Faculty Development Workshop: Faculty have also attended a long range planning and faculty development workshop held on campus. The workshop was supported through the Culture of Quality program. The purpose of the workshop was to develop faculty communication and continuity relating to the shared vision of the class.

One of the contributors to the workshop was the president of the university who reemphasized the university mission and how it related to the four-hour core requirement classes. The university physician, who is also a wellness team member, delivered the message about the important role wellness contributes to the quality, richness and fullness of life. The dialogue and discussion aspect of the workshop was facilitated by a faculty member who was not directly involved with the course. With this external viewpoint, faculty were able to converse and express thoughts and ideas in a constructive and open manner. The facilitator's responsibility was to steer and direct faculty comments and discussion in a positive direction. Prior to the workshop, faculty were asked to complete an evaluation instrument which addressed strengths, weaknesses, opportunities, and threats of the program. The open-ended survey included sections about the lab manual, fitness testing, exams, learning experiences, faculty, grading policies, class format, syllabus, and laboratory assignments. Faculty completed the survey, and it served as a valuable feedback mechanism for the long-range planning meeting. From this specific meeting several task forces (subteams) emerged. One is responsible for evaluating exercise modes and alternative learning experiences. Another orchestrates equipment and facility needs. One individual volunteered to coordinate fitness testing and activities for the disabled and special needs students.

Team goals coupled with deadlines to accomplish these course goals were generated from the workshop. With a workshop format, faculty were able to share decision making and enhance and build consensus for the shared vision of the class.

OWNERSHIP

The task forces serve as a vehicle and means to develop ownership within the overall large faculty team. When faculty members are divided into smaller task forces, the responsibility is more concentrated. Each member plays an even more important role on the smaller team. The coordinator is responsible for delegating responsibilities and for facilitating the committees. In order to keep the lines of communication open and to keep instructors informed of activities, minutes are circulated to faculty.

Through inservice sessions, general department faculty meetings, and departmental memorandums, the importance of the four-hour courses is emphasized. Faculty are cognizant of the important role they play as instructors in the success and maintenance of the four-hour general education physical education requirement. Faculty realize that the impression students receive from the life values and physical fitness course experience has a major impact upon the future of not only the four hour requirement, but also the future of the department. Through this continual reminding and enlightenment, faculty become more responsible in their classroom teaching effectiveness, professional development, and training. Periodically, the university and department missions are revisited to help keep faculty members focused on the course purposes. Through this process faculty develop a sense of ownership for the courses.

TRAINING

Since the instructional goals adopted for the wellness program can be assessed, it is paramount that the faculty have adequate training for the teaching of these goals: use of science, application of practical skills, and development and capability for life-long learning. Faculty member competencies are vital for the achievement of the goals.

Whenever new faculty members are hired, the coordinator trains them with the appropriate fitness assessment techniques and skills. Since students themselves develop competencies for self-fitness testing, and analyzing fitness strengths and weaknesses, it is imperative that faculty are competent and that the techniques are standardized among faculty. Students also obtain competencies for setting realistic fitness goals and develop and design their personal lifelong exercise plan and prescription. Faculty members must be equipped with a solid knowledge base and practical skill foundation to effectively assist and guide students through their wellness and fitness courses.

Periodically there will be special topic sessions presented throughout the year. One of the most recent sessions was presented by a professional representative who demonstrated computer software for nutritional and diet analysis. Also presented was the operation and use of accompanying interactive videos and technology for the wellness classes. Involved faculty, coordinators, and the department chair attended the session. These special topic informational seminars are vital in order for classes to be improved, upgraded, and kept current with the ever changing technology available for educational purposes.

For the Lifetime Wellness lecture class, faculty members seek out and pursue other opportunities for enrichment. We have many examples of enrichment experiences: a faculty member attended a week long seminar on alcohol and drug use on the college campus, and that extensive training enabled the instructor to be more knowledgeable and effective in the classroom. Another instructor spent several weeks in a clinical setting, in order to gain a better understanding of walking and working knowledge regarding special cases. Some of these special cases from the clinical setting that carry over into the college campus are chronic obstructive pulmonary disease (specifically asthma), spinal cord injury cases, and the nontraditional student (thirty to fifty years old).

Faculty are kept apprised of updated wellness information and innovative teaching strategies and styles through research articles, which are circulated by coordinators, individual faculty members, and the department chair. These articles are referred to periodically by faculty and are used to enhance teaching effectiveness and performance. Inservice on content areas, particularly in the Lifetime Wellness course, will be an integral part of this program.

ASSESSMENT

Assessment is an important component of the team approach concept. Without a systematic, methodical assessment and evaluation plan in place, there would be a lack of continuity and follow-up of the performance indicators and competencies achieved by the student. With a feedback data-based assessment instrument in place student competency levels can be evaluated. There are such assessment plans used for the life values and physical fitness classes.

For the fitness assessment course, randomly selected sections are targeted for the assessment samples. Faculty have played an important role in the development of the assessment instruments. By including them in the construction of the instruments, faculty develop a sense of responsibility, ownership and accountability for the course.

The assessment tool consists of an in-depth entry survey which includes sections on: 1) demographics, 2) attitudes and perceptions towards wellness, fitness and exercise, 3) wellness behavior choices (nutrition, diet, smoking, and exercise), and 4) wellness and fitness knowledge. Students complete an informed consent form and the entry survey the first day of class. Students complete the course and then, on-exit, take an abbreviated form of the survey. Students respond to exit survey questions such as: "Since I have taken this course, I can develop and design an aerobic exercise program." Students respond by using a Likert Scale of strongly agree, agree, disagree, strongly disagree.

The final exam serves as the exit instrument for the cognitive portion of the assessment. The past two years, students have demonstrated and gained competencies in behavioral areas such as making healthier food selections, exercising more during their leisure, setting realistic fitness goals, and having the tools to maintain fitness strengths and improve fitness weaknesses.

The coordinator gives the targeted assessment faculty members results of the surveys. With this follow-up, faculty gain a better understanding of their teaching effectiveness. If there is a definite weakness in the student responses when comparisons are made from entry and exit survey scores, then that area is scrutinized and evaluated. If a major concept is not grasped by the students, then teachers are encouraged to review their teaching styles, techniques, and amount of time spent on the specific concept. When the instructors are given this valuable data-based information, they become more accountable, responsible, and focused on their teaching effectiveness and the central focal point of the course, the instructional goals of science, application of practical skill and development of self-directed life long learners. Faculty develop a sense of ownership in the course when their students' competencies are reviewed.

Preassessment will be done in the one-hour activity course to determine why students are taking these classes. This will provide valuable information for instructors for further development of the classes to meet instructional goals.

Since the majority of the students complete the four-hour requirement their freshmen year, follow-up studies will be conducted to track students through their college years. True assessment for the development of self-directed lifelong learning can be achieved when the students have completed the course and are making decisions that directly affect their health, fitness, and wellness many years after the college experience. One part of the assessment will be directed at what benefit these courses have had to students during the remainder of their college career. This type of assessment can be conducted primarily through extensive alumni follow-up surveys and studies. Alumni studies give the university valuable information about the relevancy and pertinence of college courses for everyday life and help students enjoy an improved and enhanced quality of life.

CONTINUOUS QUALITY INDICATORS

To keep the courses standardized and defined, key quality indicators are developed and put in place. These continuous key indicators assure that certain systematic practices are followed throughout the course life. With the set procedures for certain courses, faculty are not "freewheeling" and losing touch with the central focal points of the course. The coordinators and department chair establish and submit the key quality indicators as accepted practices and procedures for the course.

Even though the courses are standardized and utilize common syllabi, topical outlines, textbooks, and learning experiences, faculty are encouraged to insert their personality and innovative teaching methods and styles to add their personalized touch to their class. Faculty are given the latitude and freedom to be creative and to make the learning process exciting and fun for the students and the teacher.

IMPACT OF THE LIFE VALUES AND PHYSICAL FITNESS TEAM

With the team members (instructors) centered on the purpose, goals, competencies, and performance indicators, the impact can have far reaching positive affects. Within the circle of instructors, the commitment varies with differing numbers of sections taught, translating into teaching load hours and class time required. Some instructors have the opportunity to "touch many lives" and provide students information that could "change their lives" and improve their "quality of living and wellness." Since many of the faculty are involved with diverse responsibilities such as athletic coaching, their energies and efforts may vary from time to time.

Since students are able to perform practical skills based upon science and founded research, they gain competencies and confidence in making healthier choices, fitness self testing, and enhanced overall wellness knowledge. As the students gaining these skills, they often spread the word to other students, family members, friends and the community at large. Instructors often make reference to fitness benefits for the students' college years and also the long range lifetime health benefits and risk reduction for chronic diseases. It is not unusual for students to ask the instructor's assistance to help develop an exercise program for their parents or to start a smoking cessation program. The ripples generated from the learning experiences and information delivered from these classes reach far beyond the confines of the university walls and classrooms. Figure 4 illustrates the influence the life values and physical fitness teams have on the students.

SUMMARY

Early in the process of working with the proposal to revise the general studies program, the department recognized the

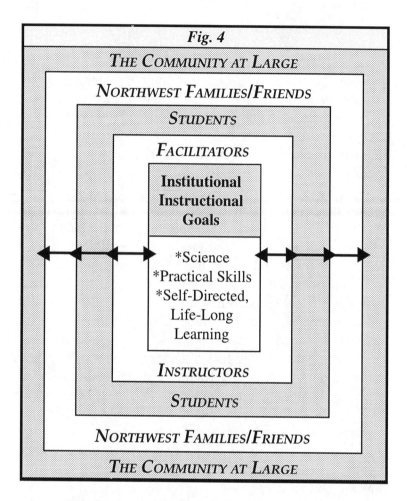

Fig. 4: Life Values and Physical Fitness Team Impact.

need to bring the faculty together in a common effort. Some of the obstacles which needed to be overcome were the traditional concept of a four-hour activity requirement, the development of the wellness approach, and the acceptance of new ideas and trends in this area of the general studies requirement. The major change which needed to occur was to have the faculty accept that this program had to become more meaningful and that it needed to have a long term effect on the students.

The transition was made easier because of the success in getting certain statements into the University mission statement and into the instructional goals and purposes (life values, well being). With the establishment of this shared vision within the faculty, it was possible to proceed to develop a consensus about how and what to do with the program. A key factor here was the agreement by the faculty in principle to a four hour requirement consisting of two hours of Lifetime Wellness, the one hour Lifetime Wellness Laboratory, and a one hour activity course requirement.

Faculty were then given the opportunity to provide input, critique suggestions, and review all aspects of the proposal. This process was significant for faculty to develop ownership of the program. All final decisions were departmental with full discussion prior to the decision-making process.

With the adoption of the core program (Life Values and Physical Fitness) by the University governance system, the process of developing the actual program began. All instructors involved with teaching the courses Lifetime Wellness and Lifetime Wellness Laboratory became a team. This involved an instructor from Human Environmental Sciences. Some structure for the Lifetime Wellness lecture course existed under the previous program and the team of faculty built on that foundation. The planning and development process for this took place over a period of a year. Course syllabi development, common assessment procedures, textbook adoption, assignments, and grading were major aspects which were addressed.

In addition, another factor which was felt to be important was the development of assessment procedures for evaluating the impact of the course on students later in their college career. A similar approach was taken to develop the Lifetime Wellness Laboratory course and to revise the activity course program. An outgrowth of this process was the writing by our faculty of a laboratory manual for the Lifetime Wellness Laboratory course and the writing of an activity course handbook by a team of faculty.

Critical to implementation of all of this is the use of faculty inservice, constant communication within the faculty, and involvement of all faculty in evaluating the program. Specific forms of evaluation are used departmentally and annual reports are filed with the University General Studies Committee to ensure continual improvement of the program. A major innovation was the assignment of coordinators to each aspect of the program. The success of the program will be determined by the value of the courses to students throughout their college

REFERENCES

Astrand, P.O. "Issues in 1966 Versus Issues in 1988." In
*Exercise Fitness and Health: A Consensus of Current
Knowledge,* edited by C. Bouchard, R.J. Shepard, T.
Stephens, J.R. Sutton, and B.D. McPherson, 29-31.
Champaign, IL: Human Kinetics, 1990.

Bouchard, C., R.J. Shepard, T. Stephens, J.R. Sutton, and
B.D. McPherson. "Exercise, Fitness, and Health: The
Consensus Statement." In *Exercise Fitness and Health:
A Consensus of Current Knowledge,* edited by C.
Bouchard, R.J. Shepard, T. Stephens, J.R. Sutton, and
B.D. McPherson, 3-28. Champaign, IL: Human Kinetics,
1990.

Shepard, R.J. "Costs and Benefits Of An Exercising Versus
A Nonexercising Society." In *Exercise Fitness and
Health: A Consensus of Current Knowledge,* edited by
C. Bouchard, R.J. Shepard, T. Stephens, J.R. Sutton, and
B.D. McPherson, 49-60. Champaign, IL: Human Kinet-
ics, 1990.

JANET K. REUSSER

J anet K. Reusser is an assistant professor at Northwest Missouri State University in the Health, Physical Education, Recreation, and Dance Department. Reusser came to Northwest in 1992 from Furman University in South Carolina. She graduated from Kansas State University with a bachelor of science in Physical Education in 1976. She received a master of science degree from the University of Nebraska—Lincoln, and a doctorate in Higher Education with a specialization in health sciences from Oklahoma State University. She is certified with the American College of Sports Medicine.

Reusser taught health education and physical education for six years in the public schools in Kansas. While in Kansas, she was also an athletic coach for several sports.

At Northwest she serves as the coordinator of the multisection Lifetime Wellness Laboratory course, teaches exercise physiology, foundations of physical education, and swimming. She oversees corporate wellness majors for field experience in the Lifetime Wellness Laboratory course. She is involved with faculty development and long range planning for the Lifetime Wellness Laboratory course.

JAMES A. HERAUF

James A. Herauf is professor and chair of the Health, Physical Education, Recreation, and Dance Department at Northwest Missouri State University. He holds a master's degree in Health Education from Southern Illinois University and a doctorate in Health and Safety from Indiana University—Bloomington.

For the past thirty years he has been teaching at the university level and prior to that taught and was a high school principal for six years. Professionally, he has been president of the Missouri Association for Health, Physical Education, Recreation, and Dance, and vice president of health for the central district of the American Association for Health, Physical Education, Recreation, and Dance (AAHPERD). He is chair of the applied strategic planning committee for the central district and chair of the quality physical education committee for AAHPERD.

Consulting with schools for curriculum development and implementation is an important part of his professional work. He is continually working with various committees at the state level for development of comprehensive health and physical education programs.

TEAMWORK

₄BUILDING
MULTIMEDIA
PRESENTATIONS

Patricia Lucido
Diane M. Krueger

❧❧ **Because results of Northwest's instructional project have continued to indicate that the multimedia presentations are a useful way to increase student comprehension in large lecture courses, additional faculty members have been invited to participate.** *❧❧*

from p. 76

W ith so many new tools and techniques available to teachers, it is an exciting time to change the traditional instructional environment. So many students are visual learners that the use of concept maps and multimedia are needed both to enhance and substitute for traditional lectures.

This chapter will describe the evolution of a faculty team dedicated to the use of tools and techniques that improve student comprehension in the sciences. The development of the project came about because we shared a concern for the quality of undergraduate teaching, as well as a desire to create a climate of student interest and enthusiasm within our respective academic disciplines.

We collaborated on a project which linked concept mapping to interactive videodisc technology in two general studies science courses: earth science and physical science. The project's objective was to measure the effect of illustrating concepts through the use of brief multimedia materials on student concept understanding.

EXPERTISE OF TEAM MEMBERS

Patricia Lucido brought to the project previous knowledge of concept maps, interactive videodisc technology, and scripting with HyperCard software. She had been working with similar projects for over five years, but had never had the opportunity to use the presentations in a large lecture setting.

Diane Krueger was teaching two large sections of the same earth science course when Lucido suggested that she use a multimedia presentation in the earth science course since several earth science videodiscs were available. Working together, vocabulary boundaries were established and concept maps designed for several key topics covered in the earth science course. The concept maps were necessary to create a framework for the interactive media and to provide an advanced organizer for the students.

CONCEPT MAPPING

Research and experience on human learning and problem solving have led numerous science educators to investigate concept mapping techniques. Based on Ausubelian psychology, concept mapping is a visual method which allows teachers and students to clarify relationships between concepts associated with a particular topic. Concept mapping is seen as a promising tool in increasing meaningful learning in the classroom. It is useful in planning curriculum, instructing students, and evaluating student understanding. We felt that the maps helped students organize the material in addition to creating the basic structure of the HyperCard Stack.

Based on the belief that people learn by relating new material to previously learned material, Ausubel suggests that concepts should be introduced which are closely tied to previously presented ideas. He refers to this process as integrative reconciliation.

Another major component of Ausubel's theory is progressive differentiation. He recommends that the presentation of new material should begin with the general and gradually progress to the more specific. Accordingly, these two processes should provide direction in curricular planning, textbook writing, and classroom instruction. This provided a rationale for use of the maps within the media presentations.

Ausubel emphasizes that the difference between meaningful learning and rote learning hinges on the ability to anchor ideas in a cognitive structure. Early in the 1970s, Novak developed this metalearning strategy to help students learn how to learn. Maps were designed to reflect cognitive structure since they show concepts arranged in a knowledge structure. Maps represent what one knows and areas one still needs to explore. The use of this tool has spread rapidly, resulting in students who have become skilled learners and teachers who become more effective (Novak, "Concept Mapping").

According to Novak and Gowin, concept maps represent meaningful relationships between two or more concepts. Concept maps show hierarchical arrangements of "concept words" which represent a regularity in events or objects. The words are linked by a verb or a connective word to form a proposition, e.g. "Plants are green." A simple concept map is

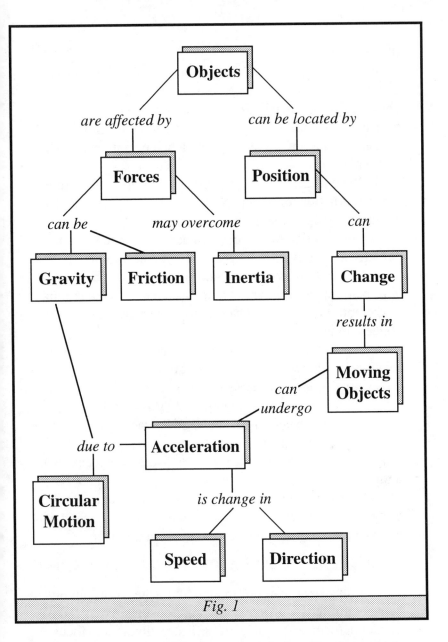

Fig. 1: A concept map which shows the relationships between terms associated with objects.

illustrated in Fig. 1.

Additional faculty members from other departments have expressed an interest in the use of concept maps in their courses. Concept maps can be seen as tools which can be used to achieve a wide variety of objectives. The following list suggests just a few possibilities which have interested other instructors:

1. Students can learn how to organize information through the construction of hierarchical structures represented by categories and subcategories.

2. Construction of a map when new topics are introduced can provide motivation for the study of a new topic.

3. Concept maps can be made at the conclusion of a unit. This map can be compared to the map made at the beginning of the unit. Students then have an opportunity to revise their concept map.

4. Since concept maps illustrate the complexity of the relationships between the concepts, discussions can be generated from differences between students' maps.

5. Although there is no single best way to organize concepts, generally students can agree on the rank or importance of concepts in the map.

6. Teachers can use concept maps to reinforce ideas about a topic.

7. Concept mapping can be used as an evaluation tool. A number of researchers were involved in the development of a concept map scoring procedure (Novak and Staff).

ISSUES RELATED TO LARGE GROUP INSTRUCTION

Learning new material in any course generally involves being confronted with new terms and concepts. When there is a concern for meaningful learning, instruction should focus on the development of personal associations between previously-learned concepts and new material. Because of the complexity of concepts in science, science educators have sought to improve instruction. As research on human learning and problem solving has accumulated, new teaching methods have been developed to enhance cognitive learning.

We were interested in creating large lecture situations which fostered more of an active learning environment versus the traditional, passive lectures. Multimedia and concept map graphics were used for short presentations that provided concept illustrations and created opportunities for student-to-student discussion and student feedback to the lecturer. These activities enhanced the students' metacognitive processes as opposed to traditional note-taking sessions.

The concept maps helped students with their organizational skills since many are visual learners. The maps showed the total vocabulary for a specific topic organized in a graphic way. Typically, students learn a plethora of terms that they are unable to link or place in an appropriate hierarchy. The maps provided one way to look at meaningful relationships between concepts and an appropriate hierarchy.

Many of the students, after years of watching television, relate well to the use of short video clips which illustrate the terminology. Although there are many fine videos and films appropriate for physical science or earth science, too often the video takes a large portion of the class period when a short video clip can be just as valuable.

Anyone who has used a number of slides in a lecture presentation can relate to the problems associated with storage, selection, and arrangement of the slides. The time involved can become a problem for instructors where visualization is critical for student understanding.

INTERACTIVE MEDIA

We had a shared vision for large lecture situations that included active learning and multimedia presentations. Too often science instruction creates a situation where terms are memorized without any real understanding. The use of "interactive multimedia" can serve to illustrate terminology in conjunction with a lecture presentation. While the traditional twenty to thirty minute film is very useful, the same major points can frequently be made with shorter multimedia displays. The project investigated the belief that students can make greater links with lecture materials if the video materials are tied briefly, but immediately, to the instruction.

The advantages of interactive video make it an ideal tool for instructional purposes. The ability to quickly access a pictorial database of photographs, graphics, and short film clips stored on a videodisc provides an opportunity to illustrate the concepts under discussion. While a concept map can supply a holistic view of the relationships between concepts, the pictures on a videodisc can be used to actually illustrate the "image" behind the words used in the maps. Elliot Eisner referred to words as "image surrogates." Words are meaningless unless a learner can relate the concept directly to a meaningful image.

EXTRA HELP

A work-study student who was employed by the chemistry/physics department became one of the project team members since she could program in HyperCard. She was able to quickly and efficiently turn the concept maps into HyperCard stacks that could drive the media presentation and provide instruction in the construction of stacks.

Obtaining Funding

Knowing that the applied research program on the campus supported a similar project in the past, Krueger and Lucido requested funding for the equipment. The proposal required a description of the problem to be addressed, objectives, methodology, evaluation procedures and a budget. The teaching station equipment is described below:

• Macintosh II si computer with 5 meg ROM HyperCard 2.1 and The Voyager VideoStack Authoring software

• Pioneer CLD-V2400 Laserdisc Player with remote control

• A VHS videotape player

• A small color monitor for instructor viewing

• A multimedia projector that accepts VGA, Mac II, or video input, and can handle four simultaneously connected input sources selected via remote control.

Implementing the Project

The first step was to enroll participants who had worthwhile contributions to make and who shared an interest in the goals of the project. Krueger was ideal for the project because she taught two sections of the earth science course which met in large lecture rooms. Since Lucido only taught one section of physical science, it was impossible for any comparisons to be made with regard to student reactions to the media presentations. It was important to involve someone with the right teaching assignment appropriate for the goals of the project.

Availability of equipment was a primary concern. At the time the team had created an interest in the future development of media presentation, there was only one computer-driven multimedia system available. The equipment had to be moved several floors to show a presentation in physical science. It took approximately twenty minutes to move the equipment and set it up for use. This created an awkward situation since there was little time to get ready before a new class of students entered the lecture room. The equipment had to be dismantled quickly to allow the next instructor ready access to the classroom.

The equipment requested in the grant was stored in one of the large lecture classrooms in order to minimize the set-up problems previously encountered. Several members of the college helped to construct a large storage cabinet to house the computer cart and projector. This provides any instructor who is teaching in the classroom ready access to the equipment and minimizes the set-up time.

STUDENT REACTIONS TO THE PROJECT

Student reaction to the use of concept maps and the multimedia lectures were obtained through surveys and reaction sheets. Presentations that ranged between ten and fifteen minutes received the most favorable reactions:

• The diagram enhances the lecture…The videos let us see how what we are discussing looks in real life.

• Sometimes it's better to see things on the screen rather than hearing it.

• It helps when the concept maps are on the screen so you can see how things are connected.

• We think the equipment is great. (The presentation) explains things in full detail and that makes it easier to take notes. We like this form of class because sitting through lecture tends to get boring.

• Makes it easier to understand because it gives examples. Makes things more interesting.

• Nice to see modern technology used. Like not taking notes and actually understanding material!

• Re-emphasized everything—helps put it into long-term memory.

A sample of the survey questions used to analyze student

reactions to the multimedia lectures in the fall of 1992 appear in figure 2. Responses were obtained from 190 students for the pretest survey, and 182 for the posttest survey.

TOPICS FOR FURTHER PROJECT DEVELOPMENT

Lucido and Krueger are interested in utilizing the multimedia presentations in other courses that they teach. And Krueger hopes to use some of the videodiscs in the collection to create several presentations for both the Introduction to Hydrogeology and Physical Oceanography courses that she teaches. She also plans to develop concept maps for several more of the main topics taught in the General Earth Science course, and will add more videodiscs to the collection in the future.

Lucido is interested in developing presentations that utilize videodiscs which illustrate teaching interactions in science methods classes. The ready access to teaching examples that illustrate specific techniques or methods would be most useful to preservice teachers.

RECRUITING NEW TEAM MEMBERS

Because the results of Northwest's instructional project have continued to indicate that the multimedia presentations are a useful way to increase student comprehension in large lecture courses, additional faculty members have been invited to participate. Large lecture classes such as biology, history and art appreciation are likely candidates for learning imagery. The enrollment process has already begun as faculty have been exposed to presentations using the equipment and have expressed an interest in learning more about its use.

There are current efforts at Northwest to design a new classroom that will be equipped with the latest computer and projection technology. The seating will afford more student cooperation, interaction and reaction to the use of the maps and multimedia.

SURVEY OF STUDENT REACTIONS
Fig. 3

QUESTION	Strongly Agree Pre	Post	Agree Pre	Post	No Opinion Pre	Post	Disagree Pre	Post	Strongly Disagree Pre	Post
My understanding of the topics taught thus far has been increased by watching the slides and videos in class.	11%	19%	60%	63%	18%	12%	9%	6%	2%	0
I understand better when I have a chance to see a picture of something as soon as its corresponding term is introduced in this course.	20%	35%	62%	52%	12%	9%	6%	4%	0	0

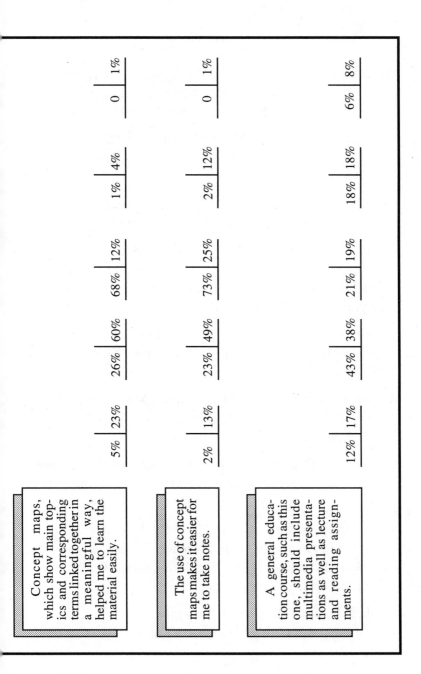

Concept maps, which show main topics and corresponding terms linked together in a meaningful way, helped me to learn the material easily.	5% / 23%	26% / 60%	68% / 12%	1% / 4%	0 / 1%
The use of concept maps makes it easier for me to take notes.	2% / 13%	23% / 49%	73% / 25%	2% / 12%	0 / 1%
A general education course, such as this one, should include multimedia presentations as well as lecture and reading assignments.	12% / 17%	43% / 38%	21% / 19%	18% / 18%	6% / 8%

Suggested Readings

Arnaudin, M. W., J.J. Mintzes, C.S. Dunn, and T.H. Shafer. "Concept Mapping In College Science Teaching." *Journal of College Science Teaching* 14(1984): 117-121.

Ault, C. R., Jr. "Concept Mapping As A Study Strategy In Earth Science." *Journal of College Science Teaching* 51(1985): 38-44.

Ausubel, D. P. *Educational Psychology A Cognitive View.* New York: Holt, Rinehart and Winston, 1968.

Karplus, R., A. E. Lawson, W. Wollman, M. Appel, R. Bernoff, A. Howe, J.J. Rusch, and F. Sullivan. *Science Teaching and the Development of Reasoning.* Berkeley: Lawrence Hall of Science, 1977.

Lawson, A. E., and J.W. Renner. "Piagetian Theory and Biology Teaching." *The American Biology Teacher* 37(1975): 336-43.

Malone, J. and J. Dekkers. "The Concept Map as an Aid to Instruction in Science and Mathematics." *School Science and Mathematics* 84(1984): 220-31.

Novak, J. D. "Concept Mapping: A Useful Tool for Science Education." *Journal of Research in Science Teaching* 27, no.10(1990): 937-949.

—. "Implications for Teaching of Research on Learning." In *What Research says to the Science Teacher,* edited by M. Budd Rowe, vol. 2, 68-79. Washington, DC: National Science Teachers Association, 1979.

Novak, J. D.,and D.B. Gowin. *Learning How to Learn.* Cambridge: Cambridge University Press, 1984.

Novak, J. D., and Staff. *Teachers Handbook for the Learning How to Learn Program*. Ithaca, NY: Cornell University, 1980.

Novak, J. D., D. B. Gowin, and G.T. Johansen. "The Use of Concept Mapping and Knowledge vee Mapping With Junior High School Science Students." *Science Education* 67(1983): 625-45.

Stepans, J. I., R.E. Beiswenger, and S. Dyche. "Misconceptions Die Hard." *The Science Teacher* 53, no. 6(1986): 65-69.

Stewart, J., J. Van Kirk, and R. Rowell. "A Tool for Use in Biology Teaching." *The American Biology Teacher* 41(1979): 171-75.

PATRICIA A. LUCIDO

Patricia Ann Davis Lucido is a science education specialist at Northwest Missouri State University in the Department of Chemistry and Physics. Her doctorate is in Curriculum and Instruction from the University of Missouri—Kansas City. She holds a master's degree in Science Education from Northwest Missouri State University and a bachelor of science degree in Secondary Education Biology from Kansas State University. Her research interests have included multimedia videodisc technology, science misconceptions and authentic assessment techniques.

DIANE M. KRUEGER

Diane Marie Krueger is an instructor in the Geology and Geography Department at Northwest Missouri State University. She holds a bachelor of science degree in Geology from Lake Superior State College and is completing a doctorate in Geology at the University of Missouri—Columbia. Her dissertation is a study of conodonts (an important Paleozoic microscopic fossil) of the Ordovician from the Ouachita Mountains of Arkansas and Oklahoma. In addition to her interest in concept maps and multimedia, she oversees student research in earth science student misconceptions and surface and ground water pollution.

TEAMWORK

5 GOAL SETTING WORKSHOPS

David C. Oehler

> ❦ **In our discussions we experienced the highest degree of collegial interaction. We found a reaffirmation of our professional ideals and regained a sense that things are working.** ❦
>
> *from p. 96*

This chapter describes a team project that was undertaken by a cross-functional group of faculty. These faculty, supported by their college dean, shared an interest in exploring the common objectives and goals of courses they taught that were offered as distributed electives in general education. A fairly large number of faculty typically teach these courses, so the project was limited to those primarily responsible for freshman and sophomore general education. The group was limited to nine people to facilitate interaction and discussion.

The presumption of distributed elective groupings, such as

those in our liberal studies curriculum, is that students obtain similar experiences independent of the specific course chosen. The historical foundation for grouping courses in distributed elective categories is tradition and the simple face validity of traditional groupings. Empirically, there is little evidence to suggest that distributed elective categories contain courses with similar objectives or outcomes.

In light of campus concern with improving the overall general studies curriculum, a summer inservice workshop was funded through the Culture of Quality program. It was held during a six-day period for faculty who teach courses in the fine arts category of humanistic studies to accomplish the following:

• Share and explore similarities of course objectives for courses offered in our distributed elective grouping.

• Share and explore perceptions of how courses offered in our distributed elective grouping address institution-wide instructional goals, ETS Academic Profile proficiencies, multiculturalism, and good teaching practices.

• Describe and define common objectives, institution-wide instructional goals, ETS Academic Profile proficiencies, and multicultural concerns on which all courses offered in our distributed elective grouping will focus (not excluding unique objectives and goals).

• Propose assessment measures to monitor achievement of common objectives, institution-wide instructional goals, ETS Academic Profile proficiencies, and multicultural concerns.

The disciplines and courses represented were:

Art Appreciation: A study of the elements and principles of art as well as forms of expression in works from the major periods of Western art. Although the works will be studied in the context of history, the course is not a chronological survey. This is not a studio course nor for art majors.

Survey of Art: A topical survey of outstanding works from

major periods of Western art with emphasis placed on the purposes of art and the roles of artists. A student having already completed a course in art history at Northwest cannot receive credit.

The Enjoyment of Music: Designed to provide the non-music major with the means to better understand and appreciate the varied styles of music. Does not count toward music major requirements.

Introduction to Music Literature: A survey of the various patterns and expressive designs found in the diverse eras of the field of music.

History of Dance: A broad perspective of the evolution of dance from the onset to the present. This course meets the fine arts requirement in the liberal studies area.

Theatre Appreciation: An introductory course surveying the aesthetic process by which plays are translated into theatrical terms and projected from a stage to an audience, including play analysis, acting, directing, scene design, costume, makeup, and stage lighting.

The workshop was structured around the following general questions:

• What objectives do our courses have in common?

• What course activities are particularly successful in achieving those objectives?

• As stated in our own academic catalogs, which institution-wide instructional goals do our courses address?

• As measured by ETS Academic Profile proficiency definitions, to what extent do our courses foster writing skills? To what extent do our courses foster reading skills? To what extent do our courses foster critical thinking skills?

• How can multicultural awareness be addressed in and by our courses?

• How can we adapt our courses for variations in the learning styles of students?

• As defined by the *Wingspread Journal's* "Seven Principles for Good Practice in Undergraduate Education," how can we maximize the teaching in our courses?

An initial concern centered on how to begin the workshop. The participants had never held cross-disciplinary discussions of course objectives and goals for general education. The goals of the first meeting were to provide common background information for follow-up discussion and to set the tone for the six-day period.

The first session was held on a Saturday and lasted six hours. The director of the talent development center presented information during the morning on the general education experimental curriculum that was being developed at Northwest, and the institutional assessment matrix. This provided "just-in-time" training on assessment practices at the institution. The director of multicultural affairs spoke to the group in the afternoon to ground the group in the current usage of the term "multiculturalism." After the presentations, the group discussed the issues which had been presented and created a statement of multiculturalism as related to their courses.

The second session was intentionally scheduled two days later in order to allow a break to digest the initial information and to reflect on the initial discussion. The session was held on the following Monday and lasted three hours. This session established the level of discussion for the remaining sessions. A statement summarizing the group's feelings regarding multiculturalism was discussed and revised. Focusing the discussion by editing this statement resulted in consensus and a sense of accomplishment. This was followed by the more difficult task of examining course syllabi and discussing goals and objectives. The pattern of beginning each session with a formal review and revision of the previous session, followed by discussing new material, was followed for all sessions.

The third session was held on Tuesday and lasted four and

one-half hours. A statement summarizing the group's feelings regarding common goals and objectives was discussed and revised. The remainder of the session consisted of discussing the following in relation to our unit's goals and objectives: the university mission, the institution-wide instructional goals, and the seven principles for good practice in undergraduate education. Following this discussion we shared assignments and activities which had been found to be particularly useful or problematic in our courses.

The fourth session was held on Wednesday and lasted four and one-half hours. A statement summarizing the group's feelings regarding the university mission, the institution-wide instructional goals, and the seven principles for good practice in undergraduate education was discussed. The remainder of the session consisted of sharing additional assignments and activities which had been found to be particularly useful or problematic in our courses, and examining and discussing the relationship between our courses' outcomes and the institutional assessment matrix.

The fifth session was held on Thursday and lasted six hours. A draft of the summary report was discussed and revised. Suggestions for assessment measures to monitor achievement of the group's goals and objectives were added to the document. Finally, a discussion was held regarding possible course revisions resulting from the workshop discussions.

LIBERAL STUDIES AND FINE ARTS MISSION

The group felt that the mission of the university as stated in the academic catalog reflected what we do in both theory and practice. In particular, we wished to endorse and reaffirm the following statements:

The University places importance on developing

each student's self-understanding, encouraging creative self-expression, and stimulating continuing intellectual curiosity. Opportunities are provided for students to develop an appreciation for the creative accomplishments of the human race as reflected in the arts, humanities and sciences. Throughout the University, students are taught to gather, organize, analyze, and synthesize information, to think coherently, and to speak and write clearly. . . [the University accepts the responsibility] to be a creator as well as a curator and communicator of ideas. . . . (Northwest, 8)

INSTITUTION-WIDE INSTRUCTIONAL GOALS

The institution-wide instructional goals which were primary to our group of courses included:

History and Government: We taught history within the context of our disciplines. We did not address the specific workings of government.

Arts and Humanities: This was one of our primary areas of focus as it is stated in the catalog:

Northwest graduates should develop an appreciation for the fine and performing arts as expressions of individual creativity and the cultures that nourished them. They should study literature, philosophy, and other areas of thought which acquaint them with the great ideas of civilization.

International and Multicultural Understanding: We believed that scholarship and teaching in the fields of art, dance, music, and theatre inherently embrace a strong multicultural perspective. Courses such as those offered in our elective category have traditionally been taught focusing on Western civilization; we felt that the broader organizing principle of examining the commonality of human experience was more suited to the needs of today's students.

For a full statement of what multiculturalism meant to the faculty in our group, including how it was incorporated into our courses, refer to Appendix A. This team-developed philosophy provided a framework for activities outside of these academic departments, including selection of guest artists, multicultural faculty in residence, and special activity programming. It was also used to help develop a campus-wide multicultural statement.

<u>Reasoning About Values</u>: Works of art stimulate the viewer to explore and define personal values. Our courses examined individuals and groups and how their interactions influence attitudes, perceptions, and behaviors.

<u>Capability for Self-Directed Learning</u>: Of particular importance to us was the development of a foundation for lifelong personal enrichment in our students. We hoped to prepare students for a life of appreciation in the theater, museum, concert hall, or wherever they encounter the fine arts as an ongoing extension of their education.

OBJECTIVES

There were primarily two objectives for the courses representing our fields of study. The first was to develop an understanding of the selected fine arts field of study. The second was to develop an appreciation for the selected fine arts field of study. Understanding must precede appreciation, as understanding provides the context for communication through the fine arts. There are several distinct facets comprising these two general objectives:

1. Each field of study in our elective grouping analyzes artistic works in terms of the elements of form, style, structure, and creativity/expression. An understanding of these elements should provide the basis for transferal of understanding

from one field to others.

2. Each field of study in our elective grouping is concerned with how artists think and communicate. An understanding of these processes is important to developing appreciation.

3. Understanding the cultural contexts within which artists create is critical to interpreting and finding meaning through artistic works. These contexts include understanding the humanistic milieu—the historical, social, political, religious, economic, and environmental influences that make up a culture, including the contributions of people from many cultures that are appropriate relative to each artistic medium. The fine arts reflect physical and metaphysical understandings of the human condition; this includes both the light and dark aspects of human experience.

4. Before the fine arts can be fully appreciated, there must be a recognition that the fine arts deal with subjective experience including other levels of reality beyond the objective. These levels of reality include, but are not limited to, the temporal world, the metaphysical world, the reality of works of art, the reality within works of art, and the levels of interpretations associated with those works.

5. The fine arts have languages of their own and deal with the subjective/interpretive expression of ideas. These languages consist of experiential communication, sometimes comprised in part by conventional language, but always including nonverbal modes of expression. Helping students understand these communication modes is a goal of our courses.

6. The fine arts explore who we are, enrich us as individuals, and by extension enrich the world.

7. We seek to create in students a capacity and willingness to express informed aesthetic opinions based on understanding, awareness, and interpretation.

ETS Academic Profile Proficiencies

One of the goals of the workshop was to consciously align general education instruction with the assessment which was being done on campus. The ETS Academic Profile proficiencies were one component of our institutional assessment matrix. In the following discussion, terms used by ETS are presented first, followed by our courses' relationship to those proficiencies.

College-Level Reading
    interpret key terms
    recognize primary purpose of passage
    recognize explicitly presented information
    make appropriate inferences
    recognize rhetorical devices

We all required reading in our courses and assumed that students possessed reading skills. We did not specifically address development of the skills listed above.

College-Level Writing
    recognize the most grammatically correct sentence
    organize units of language for coherence and
        rhetorical effect
    recognize and reword figurative language
    organize elements of writing into larger
        units of meaning

We required writing in most of our courses and viewed writing assignments as an opportunity for students to apply their writing skills to a new context as a means of clarifying thought and reinforcing learning. We did not consider the development of the skills listed above to be a primary purpose of the courses we teach.

Mathematics
    recognize and interpret mathematical terms
    read and interpret tables and graphs

evaluate formulas

order and compare large and small numbers

interpret ratios, proportions, or percents

read scientific measuring instruments

recognize/use equivalent formulas or expressions

Critical Thinking

distinguish between rhetoric and argumentation

recognize assumptions made

recognize the best hypothesis to account for
information presented

interpret the relationship between variables
presented

draw valid conclusions based on information
presented

These general survey courses do not easily lend themselves to the development of these abilities.

This section resulted in another passionate philosophical and intellectual discussion across departments. The enthusiasm generated by this discussion contributed to a desire to develop a course which could be taught through some shared format. The discussion transformed the concept of critical thinking to a personal level, where each participant understood that critical thinking was what the courses were about, but not in the terms as used by ETS. There are many types of critical thinking: linguistic, numeric, and artistic to name a few. Our courses dealt with the application of critical thinking to subjects which were for the most part nonverbal; the Academic Profile items tested verbal critical thinking skills which were not the focus of our courses. To our knowledge, there was no normed assessment instrument which tests critical thinking in an artistic context. Furthermore, the transference of critical thinking skills in our disciplines to verbal critical thinking skills is questionable within the time frame of the typical undergraduate experience. We believed exposure to multiple modes of critical thinking would ultimately reinforce and strengthen all critical thinking abilities. In order to clarify the concept of artistic critical thinking, we offer the following extensions of the terms presented above:

<u>Distinguish Between Rhetoric And Argumentation</u>: In artistic critical thinking the learner must distinguish between subject and content. The distinction was between what an artwork is and what it means.

<u>Recognize Assumptions Made</u>: In artistic critical thinking the learner must recognize the context of an artwork based on the stylistic prototypes contributing to the culture and history surrounding the artist.

<u>Recognize The Best Hypothesis To Account For Information Presented</u>: In artistic critical thinking the learner must practice problem-solving. Due to the metaphorical nature of artworks, they always present incomplete information and therefore require interpretation, selection, and creativity from the viewer. Furthermore, exact answers to questions posed by artworks are elusive at best, since one of the purposes of the fine arts is to provoke more questioning and to expand the viewer's experience.

<u>Interpret The Relationship Between Variables Presented</u>: In artistic critical thinking the learner must be able to examine commonalities and differences when confronted by multiple artworks, as well as comprehend the similarities and differences of elements within each artwork.

<u>Draw Valid Conclusions Based On Information Presented</u>: In artistic critical thinking the learner must develop constructs for evaluation based on the humanistic milieu — historical, social, political, religious, economic, and environmental influences, as well as information presented directly by the artwork.

THE SEVEN PRINCIPLES FOR GOOD PRACTICE IN UNDERGRADUATE EDUCATION

In *Wingspread Journal 's* special insert entitled "Seven Principles for Good Practice in Undergraduate Education," a "Faculty Inventory" is available as a self-assessment instrument for exploring how the seven principles are integrated into a course's design (Chickering and Gamson). We felt that the Faculty Inventory was useful for reflecting on interactions with students. However, we felt that many items on the inventory were not relevant to introductory survey courses. For example, many items deal with advisement, career planning, and student/institutional interaction. These are activities which all of the faculty members engaged in with students in upper division courses, but which none felt were universal activities in these introductory survey courses.

We reviewed all seventy items on the inventory; faculty in our group used more than seventy-five percent of the listed techniques in their survey classes, and all faculty used thirty percent of the inventoried techniques in their survey classes. Within the fine arts and humanities elective group there exist multiple courses, most taught by several different faculty members, each with his or her own teaching styles. While we found extreme commonality among objectives, the specific teaching styles used were extremely diverse. We viewed this as a positive circumstance. We recommended that the seven principles for good practice in undergraduate education not be examined through use of the Faculty Inventory. Our findings were that while we use all of the suggested activities which we felt were appropriate for our introductory survey courses, there were very few which were used by all faculty in all of these courses. Instead, we recommended sharing anecdotal information relative to the seven principles.

Core Values Within Course Content

All students are required to take one of the courses from the fine arts group. In order for meaningful communication to occur between students who have selected different courses from our group, we identified shared values.

Some of the shared values of art, dance, music, and theatre are to:

> provide aesthetic experiences
> pose questions in the mind of the audience member
> restate the crucial questions of life
> teach and to please
> articulate the dimensions of feeling
> provide a metaphorical synthesis of human experience
> explore the subjective aspects of life
> nourish nonverbal and nonlinguistic communication (sometimes in conjunction with language)
> hone problem-solving abilities
> synthesize experience, ideas, and feelings
> reflect on life experience
> enhance the wonder of the human experience
> provoke

The model of the creative process is like an hourglass—the artists funnel their experiences into the artwork which focuses the communication; the audience then applies the questions which have been raised and interprets them in relation to their personal experience.

Proposed Assessment Measures

It was our impression that researchers who construct general assessment instruments do not have sufficient background in the fine arts to construct instruments which are valid in measuring artistic objectives. On the other hand, we did not consider ourselves qualified to construct a formal assessment instrument. At the time of this workshop, we eagerly anticipated the publication of *Assessment in the Fine Arts* from the International Council of Fine Arts Deans which was released in 1994. We were disappointed by this publication, but encouraged that our own work gave us a strong basis for reconstituting assessment.

REFLECTIONS

Nearing completion of this workshop we decided to identify the primary benefits we derived from this experience. Within the academic community an attitude of skepticism and despair often prevails. In our discussions we experienced the highest degree of collegial interaction. We found a reaffirmation of our professional ideals and regained a sense that things are working. Writing and discussing helped clarify our ideas on virtually every topic; each of us reexamined our underlying assumptions about our work in our disciplines. It was refreshing to learn that we all cared deeply about general education.

The workshop fostered feelings of cooperation, understanding, and working together toward common goals. We felt that the improvement of the learning environment would occur as a natural outcome of our interactions. We truly created a Culture of Quality among faculty through this team experience.

The following summer, another Culture of Quality grant was received and eight members of the team met again to lay the foundation for a cross-disciplinary course based on the shared objectives and goals, but not focused on disciplinary issues. The organizing principles for the course were laid out, and portions are being piloted during 1995 with full implementation expected in 1996.

The Team Workshop Model

The structure of our experience was developed internally to meet the needs and interests of the participating faculty. We recommended that other groups which might undertake this process should develop a structure which is tailored to meet their specific needs. Does this process only work in the fine arts? During the summer of 1994, the process was modified and used by the department chairpersons in the sciences distributed elective category of general education. This included the departments of chemistry/physics, geology/geography, and biology.

References

Chickering, A.W., and Z.F. Gamson. "Seven Principles for Good Practice in Undergraduate Education." *Wingspread Journal* 9, no.2.

Northwest Missouri State University. "Mission Statement." In *1992-94 Undergraduate Academic Catalog*.

Appendix A
Multiculturalism as Defined by the Liberal Studies/Fine Arts Distributed Elective Courses Faculty

We believe that scholarship and teaching in the fields of art, dance, music, and theatre inherently embrace a strong multicultural perspective. Courses such as those offered in our elective category have traditionally been taught focusing on Western Civilization; we feel that the broader organizing principle of examining the commonality of human experience is more suited to the needs of today's students.

We believe that cultural diversity must be presented within the appropriate social, political, and religious contexts and not simply for the sake of trying to "be multicultural." It is our conviction that to depart from such a context and to present a particular culture or gender as "special" or "different" creates an impression that the culture/gender is less important or serious. In other words, overemphasizing the race or gender of an artist (beyond the appropriate context) creates the impression that the individual under study is a tremendous exception to the general artistic contributions of others of the same race or gender. The primary multicultural concern we see in our disciplines is to avoid as much as possible unintentional exclusion of cultures.

To this end we incorporate multiculturalism in the following ways:

• To create an appreciation and understanding for the richness and diversity within the contemporary Western heritage, we include examples showing the diversity of cultures which have contributed to it.

• To create an enriched understanding of cultural diversity, we use cross-cultural examples to compare and contrast a variety of cultural norms.

• To the best of our ability, we avoid excluding the contributions of any cultural group, and instead, strive to be culturally aware and sensitive.

In summary, we support the intentional inclusion of the contributions of people from many cultures that are appropriate relative to each artistic medium.

Appendix B
List of Faculty Participating

The following faculty members participated in creating this report:

Richard Bobo	The Enjoyment of Music
Ann Brekke	History of Dance
Chris Gibson	The Enjoyment of Music
Philip Laber	Survey of Art
Ken Nelsen	Art Appreciation
David Oehler	Theatre Appreciation
George Rose	Art Appreciation
Charles Schultz	Theatre Appreciation
Ernest Woodruff	Intro. to Music Literature

Guest Presenters:
Patricia VanDyke, Director, Talent Development Center;
    Assistant Vice President Academic Affairs
Pat Foster-Kamara, Director, Multi-Cultural Affairs
Liz Wood, Director, Counseling Center

The project was proposed and coordinated by David Oehler. Contact any group member for further clarification or explanation of material summarized in this report.

DAVID C. OEHLER

David C. Oehler is the director of the Talent Development Center at Northwest Missouri State University. He holds a master of fine arts in Theatre Design and Technology from the University of Utah and a doctorate in Higher Education from Iowa State University.

He taught in the Theatre Department at Northwest from 1982 to 1993. His responsibilities included teaching the general education survey course; teaching design and production courses in lighting, scenery, costumes, and makeup; designing for departmental productions; and supervising the costume shop.

Since 1993 he has moved to the Talent Development Center where he facilitates linkages among general education courses and coordinates assessment activities to address university program goals. He is active at both the local and state level in efforts to make assessment meaningful by providing faculty with information on student ability; in consultation with faculty teams, a variety of techniques are being designed and implemented to provide multiple measures of performance for each academic department.

TEAMWORK

6 TEAM-BASED INSTRUCTIONAL PLANNING

Georgene A. Timko
Connie J. Ury

▰▰ We care about quality library use instruction at Northwest and working as a team has helped us meet that goal. ▰▰▰

from p. 112

Prior to 1990, B.D. Owens Library at Northwest Missouri State University was a typical library with two main areas: public services and technical services. Two other areas, government documents and serials, had personnel and resources in both public services and technical services. Often, despite shared resources and personnel, there was little or no coordination between public services and technical services. Supervisors for each area forged ahead with their own agendas. When we moved toward a new management structure based upon teams and the empowerment of all employees in 1990, the tenure of the fourteen staff members was from seven to twenty-five years (with the exception of the two evening positions which turned over every two years) and the tenure of the ten faculty was from one to fifteen years. Owens was much more typical of academic libraries in 1990 than it is now, due in large part to team management.

Through team management, individual faculty and staff members were empowered to create a proactive environment. In this highly charged environment, our team-based instructional planning was a natural outgrowth. This chapter will briefly explain the team management history of Owens Library, our team structure, and how we used this structure and its hallmark emphasis on empowerment to develop our proactive library use instruction program.

The first team formed in the reference area of public services. In retrospect, the creation of a team at this time was risky because several of the key elements for successful team functioning were missing, e.g., an absence of group discussion skills, lack of training for leaders, a low level of trust, and a lack of understanding of the concept of team management. Four years later, we continue to address these deficiencies as we refine our interactive skills and develop a climate for cooperation. But hindsight also indicates that the public services area was a wise first choice because most of the participants were faculty who had the same professional education and performed basically the same kinds of assistance. This group was also held together by a common mission of public service.

After this start, other teams formed according to functional and cross-functional needs. These teams used the same ground rules which had been developed for the public services area by the Owens director. The rules were simple and based on both common sense and an intention to provide stability to the team management evolution:

- Choose a new name in order to conceptualize a new

beginning and move away from old mindsets and territorial problems. The process for choosing a name was structured as a team building exercise which allowed us to explore the function and mission of the group and provided just-in-time training in group communication skills.

• Choose a team leader. The first team leaders volunteered and were approved by the team members. Currently, we hold annual elections for each team leader position.

• Keep a record of meetings. Minutes were taken at each meeting and were published in the library's weekly newsletter.

The teams were empowered to envision projects, examine policies, and recommend actions. Recommendations were referred to the management team, called PACE, for implementation and budget considerations. Nothing that affected our daily work operations or the long term planning needs of our area was out of bounds. Consequently, one of the prime benefits of the team structure was the ownership of programs which flourished among the staff as they offered input, evaluated results and made decisions. We moved from an environment in which administrators made decisions in isolation to cooperative agreement by the people who did the work. Owens Library presently has five teams, two study groups and an auxiliary cluster. The teams are:

Distribution—circulation, reserve, interlibrary loan, periodicals, audio visual

Technical Services—acquisitions and cataloging

INFO or Information Focus—reference and library use instruction

CORe (Coordination of Resources)—collection development

PACE Management Team—partnership, adaptability, coordination and energy

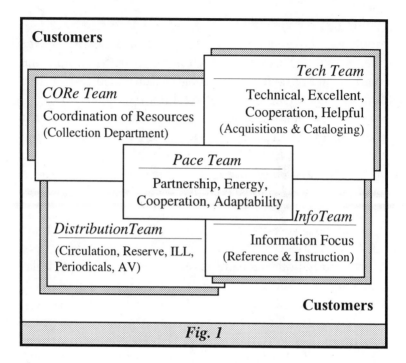

Customers

Tech Team
Technical, Excellent,
Cooperation, Helpful
(Acquisitions & Cataloging)

CORe Team
Coordination of Resources
(Collection Department)

Pace Team
Partnership, Energy,
Cooperation, Adaptability

DistributionTeam
(Circulation, Reserve, ILL,
Periodicals, AV)

InfoTeam
Information Focus
(Reference & Instruction)

Customers

Fig. 1

The teams are comprised of both faculty and staff, and for the first four years, each person served on two teams. Currently, we require participation in only one team. In our fifth year, we are attempting to bring in those who will be able to benefit from discussion of a cross-functional operation in a point-of-need model rather than taking them away from their main work responsibilities to attend a team meeting having little to do with their needs.

The PACE team consisted of elected faculty team leaders and the library director. In 1994, we added the assistant to the director of the library and an elected member of the staff to assure that we had broader representation on the management team. Either staff or faculty can lead study groups or auxiliary clusters which report to specific teams.

Since teams are so much a part of Owens, we have developed some specialized team types in order to clearly communicate with each other and handle the sorts of issues we must address efficiently. For example, we use study groups; long-term groups with specific projects to plan or problems to solve. Recommendations or solutions are presented to the team. Library Use Instruction (LUI) is the study group responsible for library instruction to university students and high school groups. It reports to the INFO team. Another study group, the Government Documents Study Group, considers the process and procedures for handling government documents received through our depository program; it reports to the Technical Services Team.

An auxiliary cluster, another special kind of team structure, is a continuing group with a single function. A member of PACE needs to be included in the group to provide communication to the management team for feasibility, coordination, timing, and implementation. This group considers a concept which would enhance the library, but is not essential to its current operation. The Virtual Information Planners is an auxiliary cluster which includes library faculty and staff as well as faculty members from outside the library. They are an advisory group which follows trends and advancements in automation so they can advise in planning for new technology.

With this background information in mind, we next examine how the Library Use Instruction Study Group undertook team-based instructional planning that incorporated partnerships with departmental faculty, the dissemination of skills in information technology, and goals in lifetime learning. This study group of the INFO team fulfills the mission of providing "innovative library use instruction." After just-in-time training, our planning procedures followed the Shewhart/Deming Plan-Do-Study-Act Cycle (Bonstingl). We applied continuous quality improvement and created the CARE (Conceive-

Activate-Rate-Enhance) cycle.

The library instruction program was conceived at a brainstorming meeting where we identified ideas that the staff has always wanted to try, and programs that we knew were successful in other libraries. Ideas generated at this initial session included:

• Creating a significant orientation exercise for first year students enrolled in Freshman Seminar classes.

• Teaching basic information retrieval skills at a point of need when a student could immediately apply the knowledge gained.

• Expanding the staffing of the library instruction program beyond the departmental liaisons to include interested library employees from all areas of the organization.

• Offering half-hour, one-on-one term paper consultations

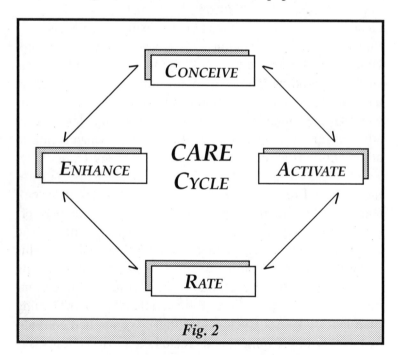

Fig. 2

focused on specific research topics to students in upper level classes.

The ideas outlined above generated the development of a tiered MEDAL—Making Education Available in the Library—Program which addresses one of Northwest's customer requirements: the development of students as lifetime learners. Each tier builds on the skills and knowledge of the previous one, and each is clearly tied to Northwest's Institution-Wide Instructional Goals, which are linked to the university's mission (fig. 3).

The goals of instruction for the Warm-Up, or Freshman Seminar component, include the students' acquisition of knowledge about basic locations of specific service points, resources, and policies of Owens Library.

Bronze Medal instruction, or second semester English composition, has outcomes which include recognition of the parts of books and periodical index citations on the OPAC (Online Public Access Catalog); ability to design a subject search strategy; recognition of the difference between a controlled vocabulary search and a keyword search; an understanding of how authority control, Library of Congress subject headings, and keyword searching each relate to our OPAC; and the ability to physically locate and retrieve books and periodicals in the library.

Silver Medal, or subject specific instruction, stresses search strategies for a discipline; an understanding of the value of authority control; appropriate keyword search strategies; and the locations and formats of specific or primary resources.

Gold Medal, or the Owens Paper PLUS (Personalized Library User Service), provides one-on-one instruction in subject search strategy for a specific topic at a point-of-need. It is available to students in upper level courses and includes personalized assistance in library research on a specific, well-

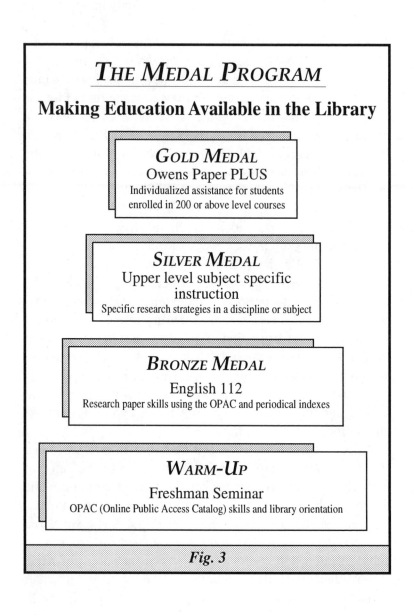

THE MEDAL PROGRAM

Making Education Available in the Library

GOLD MEDAL
Owens Paper PLUS
Individualized assistance for students
enrolled in 200 or above level courses

SILVER MEDAL
Upper level subject specific
instruction
Specific research strategies in a discipline or subject

BRONZE MEDAL
English 112
Research paper skills using the OPAC and periodical indexes

WARM-UP
Freshman Seminar
OPAC (Online Public Access Catalog) skills and library orientation

Fig. 3

defined topic. A librarian spends time discussing with the student how the research might best be approached and demonstrates the use of recommended sources.

The point-of-need concept was a significant part of our planning. Experience has shown that students will not have as much interest nor retain much information unless they are going to be using it soon (Rothstein, 25-26). If the students have a research topic along with an assignment due date, they are more apt to retain what is taught about research tools. In keeping with this strategy, all instruction beyond the Warm-Up level is delivered to students in conjunction with a specific research assignment.

Once the plan was conceived, the study group prioritized and activated the plan with a timeline. Planning for the first year of Bronze Medal Instruction began in the Fall of 1991 with a timeline of delivery in the Spring of 1992. The English 112 classes were chosen as the site for instruction because they offered a specific point-of-need in a required research paper.

We used an affinity diagram to distinguish what skills and knowledge would be identified as outcomes for each level of progressive instruction and skill building toward lifetime research competency. The six members of the Library Use Instruction Study Group and three other library staff members were recruited to deliver the instruction in the Spring of 1992 when we worked with 1,040 students in fifty-two sections.

Our third phase involved evaluating the effectiveness of the programs through written surveys and oral evaluations. Written surveys were completed by department of English faculty who also participated in the oral evaluation at a focus group meeting.

We enhanced our program by incorporating feedback from the evaluation exercises. The English faculty who suggested more hands-on practice time for the students wanted to pilot an experience in which we used three, rather than two, hours of instructional time during the Spring of 1993. Although this was a very heavy demand on our staff, we recruited additional members of the library staff to serve as "assistants" and keyboard during the demonstrations as well as to help the students during the hands-on instructional time. This practice allowed staff members who did not want to lead classroom instruction an opportunity to participate in the enhancement of the program and convey our intention to serve our patrons and meet their needs if we had the power to do so.

Since quality is a receding horizon, we continued to rate the program. Some of the English faculty provided us with feedback from their students. Written evaluations were completed by faculty for a second time. The results of this evaluation were studied by the group for continuous quality improvement, and customer-driven enhancements implemented during the Spring of 1994 included:

•To our relief, the third session for hands-on time became optional at the discretion of individual English faculty members.

•To prevent fragmentation of library public service employee schedules, we released three staff members from other public service duties. These instructors conducted all of the Bronze Medal sessions. A tour of the periodicals area was offered as an option.

•Students were more accountable for the library worksheets which were graded by library instructors before each session, and students' topics were preresearched before the second class period.

•A list of preresearched topics was provided to all English faculty allowing them to suggest a wider range of options to their students. We also extended our evaluation of the program directly to the students.

The journey toward increasing quality in Owens has been

rapid. We have used various total quality management tools to facilitate the CARE Cycle (our version of Plan-Do-Study-Act) process including brainstorming, affinity diagramming, surveys, and focus groups. We care about quality library use instruction at Northwest, and working as a team has helped us meet that goal. As it has been stated, "care must be taken to mesh service, that traditional bulwark of librarianship, with the quality, the emerging necessity in today's world, using processes that involve and empower the people who represent service and quality to their customers" (Fitch et al).

References

Bonstingl, J.J. *Schools of Quality: An Introduction to Total Quality Management in Education.* Alexandria, VA: Association for Supervision and Curriculum Development, 1992.

Rothstein, S. "Point of Need/Maximum Service: An Experiment in Library Instruction." *Reference Librarian* 257(1989): 25-26.

Fitch, D.K. et al. "Turning the Library Upside Down: Reorganization Using Total Quality Managemet Principles." *Journal of Academic Librarianship* (Nov. 19, 1993): 298.

CONNIE J. URY

Connie Ury has a bachelor of science in Education and a master of science in Education Teaching History from Northwest Missouri State University. She has been the coordinator of Library Use Instruction at Owens Library for three years and has worked at Owens Library for ten years. She received a Tower Service Award from the Northwest Student Senate during the Spring 1994 semester. They cited her for her "creativity, flexibility, and professionalism as the coordinator of the Library Use Instruction Study Group at Owens Library." She is currently vice chair of the Support/Paraprofessional Staff Council of the Missouri Library Association. Her article about the Owens Library MEDAL Program was published as a "BI Vignette" in Research Strategies in October 1994. She was highlighted in the "Supporting Staff" column of Library Mosaics in September 1994. Connie was a co-presenter at the 1994 Quad-State Paraprofessional Conference, the 1993 Academic Library Association of Ohio conference, the 1993 National Total Quality Symposium, the Nuts and Bolts of Library Instruction Workshop in 1994, and the 1994 Meeting of the Kansas Library Operations Associates.

GEORGENE TIMKO

Georgene Timko has a master's in Library Science from the University of Illinois and a bachelor of arts in History from Cleveland State University. She worked in libraries for twenty-three years, and spent the last four years as director of the B.D. Owens Library at Northwest Missouri State University where she received a Tower Service Award in May of 1993. She is currently assisting in automating the Dawes Library at Marietta College, Ohio. She was an invited speaker at the Missouri Association for College and Research Libraries Conference in May of 1994. Her workshop for the management staff at the Ramada Hotel in Omaha, Nebraska began their journey toward team management. She co-facilitated a planning retreat for the board of directors of ARK, Inc., in Parkersburg, West Virginia.

TEAMWORK

7 TEAMWORK AND PROGRAM DEVELOPMENT

David Hancock
Patrick McLaughlin
Roger Woods

❙❙ This team process encouraged each member of the task force to develop ownership in the process and become committed to its realization. ❙❙

from p. 122

What does it mean to excel? *The American Heritage Dictionary* defines excel as follows: "To be better than (others); surpass; outdo." In the fall of 1990, the accounting faculty decided to make sure that excellence would be a hallmark of their program. There were several developments taking place within the accounting profession which served as a backdrop for a complete evaluation of our program, e.g., changes in technology, regulatory requirements, and how the Certified Public Accounting (CPA) exam was to be administered. In addition, employers of our accounting students wanted us to increase students' ethical awareness, as well as their communication and analytical skills. In 1989 the Accounting Education Change Commission (AECC) had been established by the American Accounting Association (AAA) "to be a catalyst for improving the academic preparation of accountants so that entrants to the accounting profession possess the skills, knowledge, and attitudes required for success in accounting career paths" (*Annual Report*). It was clear that in order for any accounting program to keep up with all of the changes in both the requirements and the expectations of the profession, changes in accounting education were going to become necessary. All of these factors combined to indicate a different approach was needed. Within this context, we wanted to evaluate our program and be sure we were doing more than giving lip service to excellence and quality.

As a way to address these changes, and as a way to ensure that excellence be maintained within the program, the Future of Accounting Task Force (affectionately known as the FAT Force) was created by the department chair. From its inception, the FAT Force was comprised of the entire accounting faculty with each member having an equal voice, as well as an equal amount of responsibility in analyzing and implementing his or her ideas. One person was selected by the group as its leader (again affectionately known as "the Big FAT") for two years. Changing the leadership position every two years gives all members of the FAT Force an opportunity to serve in this capacity. Shared responsibility and an equal voice, critical tenents of the total quality management movement, have made the FAT Force successful and productive. Additionally, the collective pooling of the unique strengths and insights of each member has enabled the group to accomplish goals not obtainable outside of a team approach. This chapter will discuss specific strategies implemented and results of these efforts.

The first step was to conduct a self-study by looking at the program as it currently existed and making recommendations as to how we thought the program could be improved. The overall results of this self-study, called "Improving the Quality of the Accounting Program at Northwest Missouri State University," were summarized and presented to the dean of the College of Business, Government and Computer Science.

In preparing the report, each faculty member was assigned a specific area to research, and all of the individual efforts were reviewed, discussed and combined into a 14 page document. The specific areas which were researched included CPA exam pass rates, and the curriculums offered in accounting programs at other Missouri colleges and universities. The task force then developed a series of action steps which were used as recommendations to help improve the program. These recommendations included:

- strengthening the accounting grade-point requirement;
- increasing the amount of high school student recruitment;
- proposals for increasing scholarships for accounting majors;
- reinstitution of the Masters of Business Administration—Accounting Emphasis program;
- specific curriculum changes; and
- increasing faculty development activities.

This document has become the springboard used for nearly everything the FAT Force has accomplished in the past four years.

In reviewing the same document today, the team has been impressed with the fact that most of the recommendations and action-steps have been implemented. The team members agree that the true strength of the accomplishments lies in the combining of individual talents and resources. Shared responsibility has contributed to a sense of ownership by individuals, and as a result, everyone seems even more dedicated to the continued success of the accounting program.

IMPLEMENTING THE RECOMMENDATIONS

While the previously mentioned document provided the necessary framework of planning for improvement, specific methods still needed to be developed to facilitate this process, while at the same time meeting the day-to-day operational concerns and requirements. Therefore, the FAT Force established a systematic meetings schedule for addressing issues raised by the self-study as well as day-to-day issues which may result from implementing the action steps outlined in the document. This regular communication helped members maintain a sense of common purpose and kept everyone informed and focused on the task. It also allowed us to address any problems in the program which we might have been individually, but not collectively, aware of.

One result of these meetings was the changing and establishing of several departmental policies which substantially increased the strength of the program. These policies include: a) establishing two different accounting tracks: one for those students wishing to pursue a career in public accounting, and one for those wishing to pursue a career in private industry; b) establishing separate sections of Principles of Accounting: sections for accounting majors and sections for non-accounting majors; and c) requiring that each accounting major earn a minimum grade of "C" in each upper-level accounting course attempted. (The rationale and results of these policies will be discussed later on in this chapter).

Additionally, the FAT Force meetings were instrumental in the reinstitution of the MBA-Accounting Emphasis program, which had not been offered for several years. Due to budgetary constraints it was necessary to gather evidence documenting the urgent need for this program. The Missouri legislature had mandated that by 1999, accounting students must have 150 hours of college credit (the equivalent of a master's degree) in order to be eligible to sit for the CPA exam. Rather than waiting until 1999 to begin some sort of program, the FAT Force decided to be pro-active by demonstrating why it was essential to begin offering the MBA-Accounting emphasis immediately. This program will enable Northwest graduates to take the CPA exam when the legislation becomes effective and will allow us to more effectively recruit top students today.

Our proposal for reinstatement of the MBA-Accounting Emphasis was then made to the dean and other administrative leaders at Northwest.

MATRICES AS A PLANNING TOOL

As a way to visualize the program's construction and identify future needs, the FAT Force developed three matrices to be used as planning models. These matrices cover different areas of concern for the department, and as a result were specifically designed to be flexible, allowing for any necessary future program changes. At least once a year, department members provide feedback concerning what they have done the previous year which might have affected the various matrices. The annual updated compilation of each matrix allows the department to review what is occurring in the different areas, to identify any adjustments which might be necessary, and to maintain a consistent integration of technological and communication skills in each course, regardless of who is teaching the course at the time.

The Five Year Plan

"Fail to plan — plan to fail" is an old adage used quite often in business to emphasize the importance of planning. Likewise, in order to achieve our goals for Northwest's accounting program, it is essential that adequate planning take place. With this idea in mind, the FAT Force developed a model outlining a five-year plan realizing that the model will need to be updated every year to provide for the ever-changing environments of the accounting profession and higher education.

Therefore, in establishing our beginning model, the first step was to determine which major areas the FAT Force felt were the most essential to the excellence of our program. The major areas agreed upon were as follows:

- Technology Integration
- Curriculum
- Faculty
- Communication Integration
- Scholarships
- Marketing Plan
- Alumni Contacts

Second, we needed to determine specific requirements for each major area with the intent of taking appropriate action steps necessary to achieve the specific requirements. Each member of the FAT Force was asked to prepare an agenda for each category. The requirements were subsequently discussed in detail and eventually integrated into a final model which illustrates the initial five-year plan (fig. 1, next page).

The five-year plan included action steps to be taken, how they would be implemented, and the time frame. The plan was divided among the team members, who prepared a narrative for their portion based on a team consensus and/or special individual expertise in that area. Team leaders worked toward

QUALITY ACCOUNTING PROGRAM

Northwest Missouri State University
Five-Year Plan, May 1992

C=Completed   X=Proposed   P=Partially Completed

	1991-92 Fall	1991-92 Spring	1992-93 Fall	1992-93 Spring	1993-94 Fall	1993-94 Spring	1994-95 Fall	1994-95 Spring	1994-95 Fall	1994-95 Spring
Technology Integration:										
Speadsheet App'l	P	P	P	P	P	P	P	P	P	P
System App'l	P	P	P	P	P	P	P	P	P	P
Hypergraphics					X	X	X	X	X	X
Video Integration	P	P	P	P	P	P	P	P	P	P
Computerized Teaching Transparencies			X	X	X	X	X	X	X	X
Curriculum:										
"C" Avereage Required	C	C	C	C	C	C	C	C	C	C
Prin. for Actg. Majors	C	C	C	C	C	C	C	C	C	C
CPA Review Outside					X	X	X	X	X	X
2nd Auditing Course					X	X	X	X	X	X
MBA Actg. Emphasis					X	X	X	X	X	X
Ethics Integration	P	P	P	P	P	P	P	P	P	P
Faculty:										
Stipend			X	X	X	X	X	X	X	X
Development										
Stability										
Accreditation Requirements										
Communication Integration:										
Written				X	X	X	X	X	X	X
Oral				X	X	X	X	X	X	X
Scholarships:										
Freshmen					X	X	X	X	X	X
MBA Actg. Emphasis					X	X	X	X	X	X
Marketing Plan:										
Brochure					X	X	X	X	X	X
School Visits					X	X	X	X	X	X
Student Recruitment					X	X	X	X	X	X
Alumni Contacts:										
Database	P	P	P	P	P	P	P	P	P	P
Homecoming Reception	C	C	C	C	C	C	C	C	C	C

Fig. 1

Effective Faculty Teams

placing each member's portion into the final comprehensive plan. This final plan was again reviewed by each member for further refinement before being presented to the University's central administration as a way to communicate the ideas of the department.

This team process encouraged each member of the task force to develop ownership in the process and become committed to its realization. This process parallels the current business trends of empowerment to the persons responsible for the outcome of their work—a good method for successfully increasing morale and productivity.

Clearly, an individual is more likely to work towards achieving the goals of any plan if that individual is involved in the preparation of the plan. Additionally, it is also important that each individual perceive that his or her opinion and/or expertise is valued by all members of the team, team leader and administration. This has truly been the case with the FAT Force as each member's input is valued and respected, and each member feels very much a part of the process. As a result, the program has blossomed into a workable model which operates smoothly and efficiently.

The Specifics of the Plan

A. Two-Track Major. It was the consensus of the FAT Force that two adjustments in the curriculum were needed to position the program to keep abreast with the rapidly changing profession of accounting. First, there has always been some awareness that not all accounting majors want to take the CPA exam and go into public accounting; however, the curriculum had never really addressed this issue. This realization has become even more evident with the previously mentioned passage of legislation requiring 150 semester hours of college credit for candidates to be eligible to sit for the CPA exam.

Second, we found that a large percentage of Northwest's graduates take jobs in private industry. Consequently, while public accounting is the most publicized career choice in the profession, it was clear that there exists a need to prepare our students for other career opportunities, as well as to meet our student (customer) needs.

As a way to meet these needs and satisfy at least two sets of customers, both students and employers, we felt compelled to offer an alternative. Therefore, a five-year public accounting track which integrates the previously mentioned MBA-Accounting Emphasis, and a four year private industry track were developed (fig. 2 and fig. 3, p. 126-27). This alternative was implemented in the 1991-92 catalog, and the responses have been very positive from both students and employers.

B. Principles of Accounting: Majors and Non-Majors. To more adequately prepare our accounting majors for the upper division accounting courses, the curriculum was revised to offer more rigorous "majors-only" sections of Principles of Accounting I and Principles of Accounting II. This allows the faculty to concentrate on the details that accounting majors will need, such as posting to special journals, preparing adjusting entries, handling special accounting problems with alternative methods, and studying the theories behind the methodology. Also introduced into these specialized sections was a manual practice set in Principles of Accounting I, and a computerized practice set in Principles of Accounting II.

The rationale behind this separation of majors-only sections from non-majors sections was not solely for the benefit of accounting majors. Non-accounting majors have also benefited from this change, as they now can spend time on the things more important in their business careers, such as the interpretation and understanding of the financial information. Less time is spent in these sections on all of the special detail that is necessary for accountants, but not necessary for the general business person. This detail has a tendency to simply confuse the non-accountant, when such confusion can be avoided without sacrificing the critical essentials of accounting for these individuals.

Initial implementation of this facet of the plan was sometimes difficult from an advising viewpoint in regards to making both students and advisors aware of the change. Additional problems were encountered in determining precisely which material should be presented in each section. In an effort to improve and refine both the "majors-only" and "non-majors" sections, the FAT Force met weekly in the early stages to work through these difficulties. Now, while this phase has been in place for some time, it continues to be monitored on a regular basis. In fact, every semester the FAT Force looks at content, teaching strategies, and development of a common syllabus to promote consistency in all sections of Principles of Accounting.

C. Minimum Grade Requirement. In an effort to continue to challenge our current students, as well as our future students, and motivate those students to strive for excellence while working towards their full potential, the team initiated a new policy with respect to minimum grades in accounting courses. As was first stated in the 1991-92 Undergraduate Catalog, "In order to graduate with a major in accounting, a minimum grade of 'C' is required in each of the courses listed below (all upper division accounting courses), and in Accounting II." This policy has indicated to our students that we will demand more and have higher expectations of performance in all accounting courses.

D. Technology and Communication Skills. Beyond the initial curricular policy changes previously mentioned above, the FAT Force again took a pro-active approach to the quality continuum and perceived an urgent need to make a concerted effort toward improving the technological skills and commu-

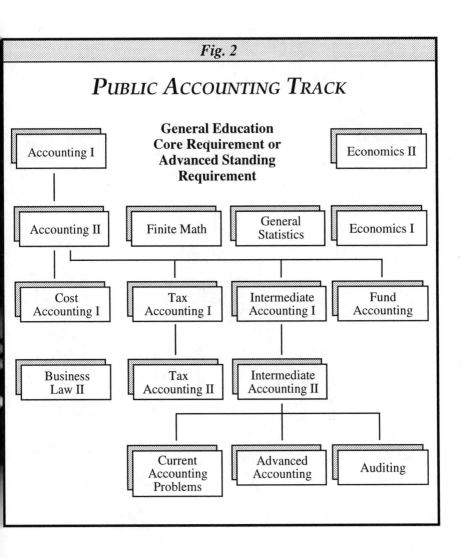

Fig. 2

PUBLIC ACCOUNTING TRACK

Accounting I

**General Education
Core Requirement or
Advanced Standing
Requirement**

Economics II

Accounting II

Finite Math

General
Statistics

Economics I

Cost
Accounting I

Tax
Accounting I

Intermediate
Accounting I

Fund
Accounting

Business
Law II

Tax
Accounting II

Intermediate
Accounting II

Current
Accounting
Problems

Advanced
Accounting

Auditing

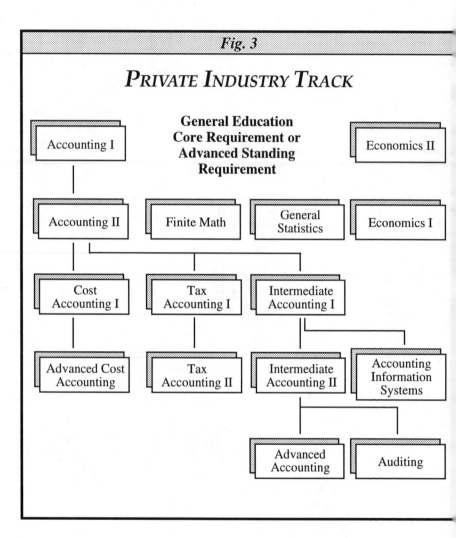

Fig. 3

PRIVATE INDUSTRY TRACK

Accounting I

General Education
Core Requirement or
Advanced Standing
Requirement

Economics II

Accounting II

Finite Math

General
Statistics

Economics I

Cost
Accounting I

Tax
Accounting I

Intermediate
Accounting I

Advanced Cost
Accounting

Tax
Accounting II

Intermediate
Accounting II

Accounting
Information
Systems

Advanced
Accounting

Auditing

Program Development

nication skills of our students.

Confirmation of this perceived need came from:

1) recruiters who indicated that most new graduates in accounting seem to lack good communication skills;

2) alumni who not only spoke of communication skills, but also indicated a need for increased usage of computer skills; and

3) the CPA exam, which recently had changed its grading criteria.

The new criteria, beginning with the May, 1994 exam, includes the grading of essay questions on <u>both</u> content <u>and</u> writing skills.

The need for improving the technological and communication skills of our students required us to look at how these skills were being taught in each of our classes at that time. Thus, the first step was to get a feel for the status quo, so that pertinent recommendations could be made to improve the program in these areas. Once again, the use of the model seemed like a useful planning tool to accomplish this task, and action steps have been set in place.

E. Technology Integration Matrix. With the substantial changes in accounting technology, integrating technology into our accounting courses became of primary importance to the FAT Force. As Northwest has been on the leading edge in this area with its totally "electronic campus," we also wanted to give our accounting program the benchmark of excellence through being a pioneer of technological implementation in accounting programs in Missouri. The FAT Force drew upon the technological expertise of its team members to coordinate the implementation of this phase of the curriculum revision. A "Technology Integration Matrix" was developed, based on what the team members felt were the most important proficiencies for our majors to possess in preparing them for their professional careers (fig. 4, next page).

TECHNOLOGY INTEGRATION MATRIX
Five-Year Plan

Courses	Systems Introduction	Exposure to Lotus	Lotus Proficiency in Acctg.	Exposure to Tax Software	Systems Analysis	Excel Proficiency	Comprehensive Systems Overview
Acctg. I	Manual Practice Set						
Acctg. II		Computerized Practice Set					
Cost Acctg.			Lotus Training/ Evaluation				
Tax Acctg.				Tax Applications			
Tax Acctg. II				Tax Applications			
Interim Acctg. I			Lotus Applications				
Interim Acctg. II			Lotus Applications				
Acctg. Info. Sys.			Advanced Lotus Applications		Flow Charting	Excel Applications	
Fund Acctg.			Lotus Applications				
Advanced Cost			Advanced Lotus Applications				
Advanced Acctg.			Comprehensive Lotus Applications				
Auditing			Lotus Applications				

Fig. 4

As indicated in the matrix, the team developed a consensus of technological goals to be implemented into the accounting program. This matrix is updated annually through the distribution and collection of a data sheet. This data sheet allows each member to provide information concerning the specific technologies utilized in each course taught, as well as specific types of software used and usage requirements made upon the students. This information is then summarized by the team leader and compared to the original matrix. A major objective of this process is to ensure that as teaching assignments, objectives and technology change, the necessary proficiencies are still offered throughout the entire accounting program. While the team does not direct what method should be used to promote any proficiency in any specific course, recognizing each instructor's right of academic freedom, it does ask each member to follow the matrix in the interest of maintaining a consistent approach to this technological integration.

One example of technological usage was in the 1993-94 school year, in which several team members began using laser disc technology (for computerized transparencies, learning objectives, definitions, problem examples, and mini-cases) in two of our principles courses on an experimental basis. Additionally, Northwest became one of the first colleges in Missouri to use hypergraphics technology in our accounting classrooms. Under the hypergraphics system, which includes individual student response pads, student participation and interaction in the classroom is substantially increased. This, in turn, enhances learning and gives instant feedback to both the student and the instructor on each phase of the material being presented. Once again, empowerment and the ability to utilize our team members' strengths allowed for this type of program development, which helps satisfy the needs of our internal and external customers.

In addition during the fall of 1992, the department decided to move money from other departmental budgetary areas and apply those funds toward the purchase of the Commerce Clearing House CD-ROM Tax References in an effort to make further improvements in the area of technological integration. While this was expensive, it further demonstrated the willingness of all individuals within the department to forego purchasing other necessary items, because it benefited the overall program, resulting in our students having access to a complete set of tax references, as well as the use of state-of-the-art technology in the area of tax research, which obviously will provide them with very valuable and useful experiences for their future careers.

F. Communication Matrix. Accounting has become a profession which requires its members to be much more than "number crunchers." The stereotypical social recluse, equipped with thick glasses, green eye shades, pocket protector and calculator, is an image of the past. In order to succeed in today's professional world, the accountant must be an effective communicator, utilizing both written and oral communication skills. As a way to guarantee that a wide range of communication skills are being offered to each student throughout the accounting program, a communication matrix, similar to the aforementioned technology integration matrix, was developed (fig. 5, following page).

The process regarding implementation and integration of the communication matrix is identical to the process for the technology matrix. Again, the success of this process is dependent on the full participation and cooperation of every member of the task force team and has been accomplished through the positive attitude of doing those things necessary for the good of the program.

Fig. 5

INTEGRATION OF COMMUNICATION SKILLS IN THE ACCOUNTING CURRICULUM
1992-93

Course	Oral Report	Oral Discuss	Written Research Report	Written Article Summary	Written Case	Term Paper	Essay Exam Quest
Acct. I							X
Acct. II		X			X		X
Cost Acct.							
Tax Acct. I		X	X		X		
Tax Acct. II		X	X		X		X
Int. Acct. I							
Int. Acct. II				X	X		X
AIS	X			X	X		X
Fund Acct.		X		X		X	X
Adv. Cost Acct.		X		X	X		X
Auditing					X		X
Adv. Acct.				X			X
Manag. Acct.	X	X			X		X
Bus. Law II		X	X	X	X	X	X
Cur. Acct. Prob.							X

Obviously the FAT Force's efforts required many hours of meeting, discussion, and exchange. Initially, the meetings were to be held on an as-needed basis, which consisted of once every two to three weeks. However, as the scope and importance of what was being accomplished grew, so did the need for more regular meetings. Even with regular weekly meetings it became evident that more time was needed to sufficiently discuss all the ideas and contributions being shared by team members. As a solution to this problem, the team decided to designate an entire day as a "FAT Force Retreat" to cope with these various issues.

A full agenda of items to discuss was developed by the team leader, made up primarily of those things which needed prolonged, thoughtful discussion, but which would be difficult to fully cover during a regular meeting. This agenda was distributed to each member before the retreat, allowing for some preparation by individuals to facilitate more meaningful interaction among team members.

This became an integral part of the model implementation process. With time to interact with the entire team, many issues surfaced and were discussed. Some of the areas covered varied from very general, such as individual ideas, goals and teaching strategies, to specifics such as teaching loads and textbook selection. This forum for exchange—a process of shared decision making—has developed into an annual event which the team now calls an in-service day. Perhaps surprisingly, it is now even eagerly awaited by all FAT Force members, in that it enables us to determine the needs of our students and their future employers, both of whom we consider to be our very important customers, and allows us to develop successful strategies to satisfy both groups.

The following is a representative sample of the results

which have been achieved from these in-service days:

• the implementation of the study of ethical issues in all accounting classes, to include the purchase and use of an ethics handbook. This handbook is introduced in Intermediate Accounting, with the same handbook used in nearly every other subsequent class as each individual instructor believes appropriate;

• the development of an alumni survey, alumni data base, and an employer survey to assess our success in meeting the needs of our customers, our students and their future employers, as measured by the four "key quality indicators" developed by the department; and

• the establishment and development of a strong recruiting program, to include the design of an attractive departmental brochure, the introduction of accounting scholarships for in-coming freshmen, and the recruitment of high school seniors through visitation and presentations to area high-school accounting classes.

Again, each of these specific accomplishments were under the direction of, or completed by, individual team members of the FAT Force, with input from all other team members. It is the total participation, as well as cooperation of all members of the Force, that has made this effort so successful.

CONCLUSION

Our goal was not to simply model our program after one that some other school may feel is successful, but rather to take some of the standards that others use as a measure of success, add them to the goals and objectives that we feel are imperative for the success of Northwest students, and then build our accounting program by incorporating these benchmarks. To emulate some other program as our benchmark might prevent our department from achieving our goals, due to the vast differences in resources available and individual missions in the various accounting programs throughout the state. We continue to strive to make our program, as we proceed with the implementation of our action steps, meet not only the educational needs of our customers, but also to be classified as one of the truly excellent accounting programs anywhere.

From the discussion contained in this article, we hope it is obvious that each member of the FAT Force is genuinely committed to developing and maintaining a truly excellent accounting program. But in order to achieve this success there are two very essential requirements for our efforts to continue to succeed. First, as has been emphasized throughout this article, total team participation and cooperation is essential. Each member of the FAT Force has demonstrated a willingness to put individual desires aside for the overall good of the program. Without this kind of cooperation, it would be impossible for this team effort to succeed.

Secondly, the FAT Force has enjoyed the total cooperation of this process by the administration. Through this cooperation and empowerment, decisions have been made by the individuals most responsible for their implementation, as well as by the individuals who work most closely with the students to evaluate the value of these efforts. It is with a deep sense of gratitude that the FAT Force acknowledges and appreciates this degree of empowerment granted to them.

The initial five-year plan was an attempt to establish an ongoing process of continuous quality improvement. This ongoing process is designed to maintain and reinforce the attributes that make our program excellent. As indicated in figure 6 (next page), the updated five-year plan clearly demonstrates the team's commitment to this ongoing process. Certainly this plan is not viewed as an end result, but rather as a planning model to help us continually improve and excel.

QUALITY ACCOUNTING PROGRAM
Northwest Missouri State University
Five-Year Plan, May 1993

C=Completed, X=Proposed, P=Partially Completed, O=Ordered,
Y=Proposed Completion

	1991-92 Fall	1991-92 Spring	1992-93 Fall	1992-93 Spring	1993-94 Fall	1993-94 Spring	1994-95 Fall	1994-95 Spring	1995-96 Fall	1995-96 Spring
Technology Integration:										
Speadsheet App'l	P	P	P	P	P	P	P	P	Y	Y
System App'l	P	P	P	P	P	P	P	P	P	P
Hypergraphics					O	P	Y	Y	Y	Y
Video Integration	P	P	P	P	P	P	P	P	P	P
Computerized Teaching Transparencies			X	X	P	P	P	P	P	P
Curriculum:										
"C" Avereage Required	C	C	C	C	C	C	C	C	C	C
Prin. for Actg. Majors	C	C	C	C	C	C	C	C	C	C
CPA Review Outside					C	C	C	C	C	C
2nd Auditing Course					P	P	C	C	C	C
MBA Actg. Emphasis					C	C	C	C	C	C
Ethics Integration	C	C	C	C	C	C	C	C	C	C
Faculty:										
Stipend Development Stability			X	X	X	X	X	X	X	X
Accreditation Requirements			X	X	X	X	X	X	Y	Y
Communication Integration:										
Written				P	P	P	P	P	P	P
Oral				P	P	P	P	P	P	P
Scholarships:										
Freshmen					X	X	X	X	X	X
MBA Actg. Emphasis					X	X	X	X	X	X
Marketing Plan:										
Brochure					P	C	C	C	C	C
School Visits					P	P	P	P	P	P
Student Recruitment					P	P	P	P	P	P
Alumni Contacts:										
Database	P	P	P	P	P	P	P	P	P	P
Homecoming Reception	C	C	C	C	C	C	C	C	C	C

Please note that at the time of publication the 1994 update was not complete.

Fig. 6

We believe that during the last four years, the FAT Force has demonstrated that a teamwork approach to program development is very effective. The total cooperation of the team members, along with the cooperation from the administration, has allowed for the implementation of sound policies and procedures, which have substantially improved the accounting program. The use of an overall model and various matrices as a planning guide will encourage a constant focus on the future, insuring that the program will remain current and on the cutting edge of the accounting profession. The continued cooperation by everyone involved, along with the continued use of this model, will guarantee a program of excellence as we meet the challenges of the twenty-first century.

References

Accounting Education Change Commission, American Accounting Association. *Annual Report 1989-90.*

The American Heritage Dictionary of the English Language. 1979 ed.

Northwest Missouri State University. *1991-92 Undergraduate Catalog.*

DAVID
HANCOCK

Biographical Sketch

David Hancock is an instructor of accounting and is a Certified Public Accountant. He began teaching at Northwest Missouri State University in 1982, taught business for five years at Tarkio College, and then returned to Northwest in 1990.

David received both of his degrees from Northwest, graduating with a bachelor of science in Accounting in 1980, and a master's in Business Administration— Accounting emphasis in 1982. He is a member of the American Institute of Certified Public Accountants, the Missouri Society of Certified Public Accountants, and the Missouri Association of Accounting Educators.

PATRICK McLAUGHLIN

P atrick McLaughlin is an associate professor and chair of the Department of Accounting and Finance at Northwest Missouri State University. He earned a bachelor of science in Business Administration from Central Missouri State University and a Juris Doctorate degree from the University of Missouri — Kansas City.

He has taught business law and insurance courses at Northwest for the past seventeen years. In addition, he works as the Nodaway County Assistant Prosecuting Attorney, City of Maryville Prosecuting Attorney, Tarkio Municipal Judge and owns his own private civil law practice.

ROGER WOODS

Roger Woods is an instructor of accounting at Northwest Missouri State University and a practicing Certified Public Accountant.

He holds a bachelor of science degree from Nebraska Wesleyan University and a master's in Business Administration from Northwest. He has been teaching at Northwest for thirteen years and prior to that worked for twelve years in public and private accounting.

Woods continues to work in public accounting and is a member of the American Institute of Certified Public Accountants, Missouri Association of Accounting Educators, and Institute of Management Accountants.

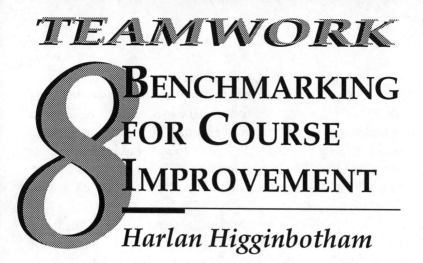

TEAMWORK

8 BENCHMARKING FOR COURSE IMPROVEMENT

Harlan Higginbotham

> ❦ The fact that we researched, benchmarked, and planned for several years while trying to gather funding for the computer lab project worked to our advantage in the long run. Because we did not jump at the first option that presented itself, we were able to get a better, more efficient, and more flexible system. ❦
>
> *from p. 152*

It's morning, and you are walking down a long hall that connects with a row of university classrooms. Most of the doors to the classrooms are closed, but ahead you see one propped open. You hear soft clicking noises and an occasional subdued voice, or a muffled but exuberant "Yes!" emanating from the room. Your curiosity aroused, you pick up your pace a bit, hoping to discover what's going on inside that room. As you approach the door, a bell rings in the distance, and you hear books being gathered, chairs being moved around, students hurrying out of the room and on to their next class. Three students crowd out the door together. "Hey, that was fun!" says one, and another adds "I want to stay, but I have to get to my art class." The third interjects, "Well, I want to see what happens next—I'm coming back after my last class this afternoon."

Does that scenario sound like a dream? What if the open door led to a chemistry lab, and the three students leaving it were not chemistry majors? "There are always a few students who truly enjoy the required classes outside their major field of study," a person might argue. But in the case of the newly installed, computer-assisted chemistry lab at Northwest Missouri State University, positive reactions to laboratory experiments, such as the three described above, are the rule rather than the exception.

BENCHMARKING AND RESEARCH

Northwest's chemistry lab improvement efforts started back in 1984, the first year the university Computing Committee heard about some schools in the region that were using computers for various educational purposes. We visited Union College in Lincoln, Nebraska, to examine their electronic campus, and the University of Nebraska in Omaha, which was manufacturing documentary videodiscs for educational use.

The trip to Union College convinced the visiting team that an electronic campus at Northwest would be possible. As a result, when we traveled to the University of Nebraska later that same day, we were already envisioning our campus as an environment that would, technologically, lend itself well to computer-aided instruction. At the University of Nebraska, we examined the first truly good work with videodiscs. The discs allowed accurate, random rapid access—in other words, you could select and go to a particular segment or image in a matter of seconds—which had not been possible with videotapes. These early videodiscs could be used for showing a series of short film clips to accompany a classroom lesson. We became convinced that videodiscs could be used effectively in the classroom as aides to instruction. That visit served as the first "benchmark" for our chemistry computer lab.

Then in 1987, the first chemistry software was issued on videodisc, and it was interactive, allowing students to interact with video images to control, design, and change the experiments being performed. It could be used for tutorial sessions, classroom instruction, or individual computer-assisted instruction.

This software was in use at the University of Illinois at Urbana-Champaign, where it was authored by one of their professors, Stan Smith. When the committee visited the college, we spoke with many of the students and all faculty involved in using the software. We then spent the better part of the day in the general chemistry laboratory to observe the technology for ourselves. After examining this laboratory, we knew we had found our model.

At that point, our chemistry department decided to preview the first edition of the chemistry software by purchasing a videodisc (the software), and borrowing a videodisc player (the hardware) from our own computing sciences department. It was first tested in the summer in a small section of general chemistry for non-majors. Because we had only one machine for the videodisc, we were unable to use it in classrooms department-wide. After testing the videodisc system, the committee became convinced that it could provide effective chemistry instruction, if the university could purchase enough sets of hardware. One or two workstations would be inadequate for instruction in a large class.

Acquiring the New System

After we returned from the University of Illinois, we demonstrated the interactive chemistry software for the vice president of academic affairs and the president by conducting a gas laws experiment using first traditional and then the interactive videodisc methods. The demonstration was a success — we did not spill any mercury on the floor with the computer-assisted method. Both administrators were convinced that computer-aided instruction in the laboratory was a logical next-step for Northwest's electronic campus.

Along with the decreasing costs of personal computers, the development of a new version of the software that did not use videodiscs lowered the costs of the system and helped us more easily realize our goal. The new software had replaced videodiscs with CD-ROM technology. The main advantage of the CD-ROM is that it does not require a separate player for each workstation; a player is only needed once, to load the disc contents onto the network's hub, the server machine's hard disk. After that, students access any lesson or experiment through the computer at their lab workstation, which ties into the network. The CD-ROM version is thus much less expensive in a networked system than the original videodisc version.

Implementation of the New System

Beginnings

The CD-ROM computer chemistry/math lab became operative in the fall of 1993. Not all the teachers used the computer lab at first; only two chemistry courses started using the computer lab immediately. We didn't want to force it on anyone. However, we encouraged instructors who wanted to use it to do so. With each new semester, more teachers have incorporated the computer lab into their courses. The computer lab does not replace the wet lab; it enhances it. We still strongly believe that students need to have hands-on experience with the equipment and the materials in the wet lab in order to be thoroughly educated in chemistry.

While they are designed for general chemistry, many of these computer-aided chemistry experiments can also be incorporated into upper level courses. This past year, instrumental analysis and analytical chemistry used the computers to a limited extent. Organic chemistry uses the computer lab quite a bit now, as does physical chemistry. Eight or nine chemistry courses use the new lab to some degree. Of course, the general chemistry labs use it most extensively, and the math department uses it for calculus on a regular basis.

When using the computers for a lab course, the instructor creates a tailor-made menu for each course from the list of the software's available lessons and experiments. The instructor can even assign a deadline for individual experiments, so that they must be completed by a certain date in order for the computer to "count" them as completed assignments. When students sign on to the computer, they indicate which course they are in, and the appropriate menu appears on the screen. As long as the assignments have been made (i.e., added to the course menu by the instructor), students can complete them at their convenience, working ahead to accommodate their own schedules if necessary.

As the student completes a lab, the computer makes note of it: a check mark denotes completion of the assignment, and a dash indicates that the student has only partially completed the lab. The computer keeps track of what each student has done. In this way, the student has a record of his or her completed assignments, and the instructor, by accessing the master account, can look at what all the students have done. The opening screen tells the instructor how many experiments each student has finished, when they were last on the computer, and how long they spent on the computer. The instructor may also request to see an individual student's record in greater detail; the detailed screen shows a list of the actual labs a particular student has completed or partially completed. There is also a way for the instructor to, at any time, check to see which computers are free, which are in use, who is using them, and what lesson is being worked on. The instructor can also ask for a printout of any of the available information.

IMPROVEMENTS ON THE BENCHMARK PROGRAM

In implementing computer-assisted instruction in the Northwest chemistry lab, the first improvement we made on our benchmark model was to standardize our hardware. The University of Illinois's lab housed a hodgepodge of hardware, and used multiple generations of the chemistry software in one lab. As a consequence, students performed the same experiments, but they used a variety of equipment to complete them; one group of students might be working on videodiscs, while another group might be using CD-ROM. Possible complications can develop in this situation. For example, if there are a variety of machines to operate, there will always be some students who are familiar with only one type of machine. If the available machines of that type are in use, those students will have to wait, even if there are open machines of another type. At Northwest, all the machines are the same, so students can use any open station.

We also changed the way the computers are physically arranged in the work area. At the University of Illinois they used a carrel design (fig. 1). This design gave each student a private computer area, but left very little room for anything else; note taking was difficult. The PCs were placed on each carrel's tabletop, with the viewing monitors (as usual) set slightly above a straight sight line, which meant that students had to tilt their heads back slightly to look at the screen. A common complaint of PC users is neck pain brought on by holding their heads in an inclined position for hours on end; such pain can encourage a negative response to using the computer lab. The carrel design also was not conducive to group interaction (i.e., group discussion or lecture before, during, or after a lab period). We had seen advertisements for a pentagonal carousel type workstation, in which the workstations were circularly grouped by fives (fig.2), but this design, while perhaps more aesthetically pleasing, solved none of the carrel's problems and was even more inhibiting to group interaction.

Here at Northwest, computers are placed beneath long worktables, with the screens visible through a clear tabletop and placed at a comfortable viewing angle (fig. 3). The in-the-table design makes the worktable quite versatile. It can be used as a table (for note taking or figuring) when necessary without the computer itself getting in the way or reducing the available workspace. Faculty-group interaction is not inhibited, either, since students sitting at each workstation have a clear view of the front blackboard and podium. If the laboratory instructor chooses to incorporate group discussions into the lab experience or give instructions before the students begin a particular lesson, the computer workstations will not get in the way. In addition, each station is equipped with a portable "hood" that can be placed as a shield or divider around the clear section of the tabletop, so that students may work privately. Some people feel inhibited if they think others are watching what they are doing. The in-the-table design thus eliminates the neck-strain problem and makes it easier for students to take notes, without sacrificing the security of a private workspace.

A third change we have implemented involves the assessment of students' learning. When we visited the University of Illinois, the students there completed computer experiments,

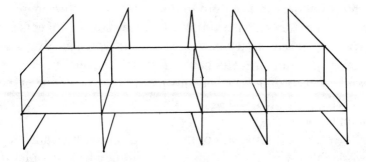

Fig. 1

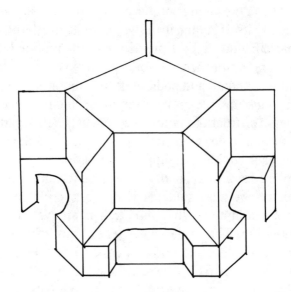

Fig. 2

Benchmarking for Course Improvement

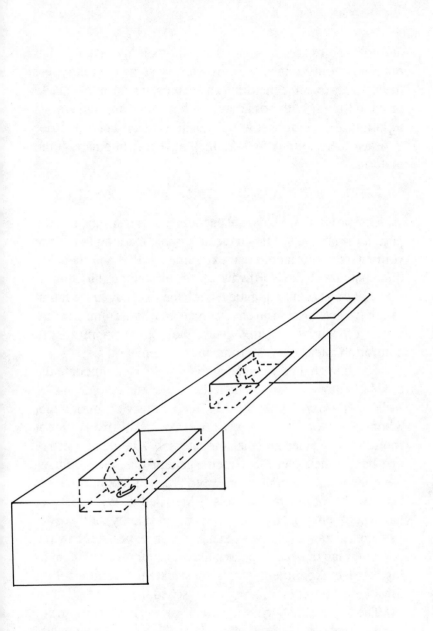

Fig. 3

and took notes if they wanted to, but were tested over that material in only some cases. At Northwest, we regularly test the students over the material, and in most instances also have provided them with some sort of reporting mechanism—a report to fill out, or follow-up questions to answer—in order to assist them in making sure they have a firm grasp on the material.

CHANGES IN OLD SYSTEMS, NEW PROBLEMS

One problem we have not encountered is resistance on the part of the students. They have no trouble learning to use the computers to do laboratory experiments. Perhaps their acquaintance with the Northwest electronic campus has simplified that transition, or maybe it has been aided by the fact that they have grown up in an environment in which computers are a part of daily life. Either way, the computers provide a comfortable learning environment for them.

The first change we needed to make to accommodate the new laboratory, it was decided that we would convert the ag soils lab into a computer lab. This means that we now conduct laboratory experiments for a given course in two different rooms—the wet lab and the computer lab. About one-third to one-half of the experiments in the general chemistry courses are done in the computer lab. Both types of laboratories are important to a student's chemistry knowledge. While the wet lab experiments and the computer are not side-by-side, we do, in some instances, have students do an experiment in the computer lab that teaches them the procedures for an upcoming wet lab experiment, which means students and teachers must keep up with a rotating room schedule.

The second change we had to make was to delete some of the wet experiments from our course syllabus. In order to add new experiments to a course plan, instructors have to eliminate old ones. And of course, some experiments take a longer time to complete in the wet lab, so instructors must take the time factor into consideration as they plan. Creating an effective course of study is, by nature, an on-going process. For example, in my own classes I have used a lot of trial and error in deciding how to combine the two types of laboratory experiences. Although I am in my second year of using the computer in the classroom, my syllabus is still in flux. This is not a huge problem, but it does increase the time it takes an instructor to organize a course.

Thirdly, laboratory scheduling has changed rather dramatically. The first year, classes met in the lab according to a strict schedule—it was very structured, similar to the traditional type of wet lab scheduling. But that was before the computer management system became operational; the system was installed with an incorrect type of board for networking, so it took nearly a year for everything to be adjusted. But now that the computer management system is operational, more flexible scheduling is an option. The management system allows for individual-course menus, so students can use the computers whenever they want and can work at their own pace—their assignments are right on the computer. For example, students may have an entire week in which to complete a laboratory. This does not mean that students are thrown adrift in the computer lab, to sink or swim. Instructors monitor the computer lab during their scheduled lab period, and students know they can receive help then if necessary.

In the interest of security, the chemistry/math computer lab is open only when we can schedule a monitor, which works out to a total of forty-four hours during the week. During those hours, any chemistry or math student may use the lab. The math department has the exclusive use of the computer lab an additional eight hours a week (a calculus class is actually taught in the laboratory, using the computer system). We select responsible volunteers to act as monitors in the lab—

math and chemistry faculty, graduate students and even some upper-class undergraduates. Because the software is so user-friendly, monitors do not have to be computer experts, just good supervisors. Many people have helped out by volunteering to be monitors. Ideally, to allow students the greatest self-scheduling flexibility, the lab would also be open on Saturdays, but we have not yet been able to arrange that.

Opponents of a computer lab might insist that this system carries with it a great potential for falsified assignments. Even using the computer's management system, all you know for sure is that someone, using the student's password, has signed on to the computer and done the work. We do not deny that, in this type of lab, there is the potential for cheating. However, in order to discourage any attempts at computer lab plagiarism, students are regularly quizzed over the computer lab material. It is then in the students' best interests to actually do the work themselves.

Benefits to the Quality of Instruction

In the past, science teachers have not been able to guarantee students success in laboratory experiments. Many students can spend three hours in the wet lab—setting up equipment, measuring compounds, observing a reaction—and in the end, sometimes due to only minor errors in their procedures, they come out of the lab wondering, "Why did I do that experiment? It didn't show me a thing! I wonder what was supposed to happen?" Unfortunately, it is impossible for one instructor—who has, of course, only one pair of eyes—to catch every procedural error made by the thirty-five to forty students in a laboratory class. This situation is frustrating for both students and teachers, and it negatively affects the overall quality of the learning experience.

The major benefit of learning chemistry in a computer

laboratory is that students can be guaranteed success. Students won't make the mistakes on the computer that will lead to poor results on experiments because the computer itself will watch and help them every step of the way. Instead of students' being completely lost, the computer will make them aware of errors and give them a chance to try again before continuing with the experiment. In this way, computer-assisted instruction ensures that each student receives non-stop individual attention. The computer acts like a teacher's assistant: it keeps an eye on what students are doing, tells them when they have made a mistake, and informs them that they must redo a part of the experiment until they have achieved the desired result, taken an accurate measurement, or collected enough data. This means that students will learn more and gain confidence. In addition, it frees up the instructor to help students individually on more complex matters, such as understanding the concepts behind the experiments.

Another way the computer lab improves the quality of the learning experience is by increasing laboratory safety. Safety is a real problem in a traditional wet lab due to the handling of toxic materials that can be dangerous. With the computer lab, the risk for injury is reduced, and new, simulated experiments that were prohibitively dangerous in the traditional lab can also now be included.

The computer lab can also have a positive environmental impact. In a traditional chemistry lab, toxic materials are generated. Years ago, the solution used to be to blow those materials out the exhaust hood and let them disperse into the air we breathe. We have progressed, in recent years, and now try to minimize the amount of toxic materials we generate in the wet lab. Our computer lab will help by further reducing the toxic materials we produce. Certainly, students, faculty, and administrators can all benefit from participating in this way to help keep our environment clean.

The computer lab also benefits students by allowing them a greater range of laboratory experience than they could encounter in the same amount of time in the wet lab. In the study of gas laws, for example, the experiments are much more thorough with the computer simulations than they could be in an actual situation. The rates-of-reaction experiment provides another example—students are able to closely follow the rates of reaction with the computer but would not be able to do so in a traditional lab. In addition, the time required to perform an experiment is compressed in the computer simulations. You do not have to walk across the room to look for model A, and then look somewhere else for model B—the equipment appears immediately on the screen. The compression of elapsed time increases the amount of experimentation you can do. In one experiment on air analysis, students go out in the field and collect air samples from different places, then bring them back to the laboratory for analysis. That experiment takes a full week to complete in the traditional way, but only takes a few hours when you convert to the computer-simulated lab. With the computer, travel time is saved, and packing and unpacking the sampling apparatus is no longer necessary.

The computer lab also makes laboratory preparation more efficient. Solutions do not have to be prepared and dishes do not have to be washed for the experiments simulated on the computer. Most large universities have a stockroom person who checks equipment in and out, makes sure it's clean, keeps materials in stock, and prepares solutions for experiments. Here at Northwest, we have never been able to afford a stockroom person, so faculty are responsible for all those duties. Because there are several faculty, the procedure is not as efficient as it might be—imagine five professors all trying to prepare the same labroom for their different courses. For the simulated labs, then, the computer itself becomes the stockroom person. Computer-simulated labs can particularly help out at small universities where stockroom duties are likely to be less streamlined.

We also gain an advantage from this kind of laboratory in equipment costs. In simulated experiments, students do not use actual equipment, so there is less wear and tear on the school's everyday lab equipment (test tubes, beakers, burners, etc.). In addition, some experiments require special equipment—equipment that we do not have to buy if the student does the simulated experiment instead. In the past, there were many experiments we could not do because of a shortage of equipment that we are now able to do on the computer. Of course, computers cost money, too. We probably will not break even on the costs at this point—installing a computer lab involves a huge investment at the outset. But we hope the computers will last longer than, say, a test tube.

Assessment of the New System

At this early stage in the use of the new computer lab, we lack statistics about how effective it is. However, we do know that the students like it. We receive very little negative feedback from the students about the computer lab, but do hear a lot of positive feedback. That fact alone tells us the chemistry/math computer lab improves the quality of our students' learning experience. Although we have not yet done an in-depth analysis of it, one member of the department is currently conducting research to determine how effective the computer chemistry lab is as a teaching tool. In the future, we hope to have more factual data to support our intuitive response.

Reaching Out to Others

It is natural for people to talk about successes in their lives, and we at Northwest have certainly talked about our new computer lab. Most educators in our region have heard about it. As a matter of fact, our sister institution, Missouri Western State College, in St. Joseph, Missouri, sent their chemistry department and university vice president up to look at it—they were very impressed. We do not know if they have plans to install a computer lab or not, but we know that they liked what they saw. They probably felt about the same way we did when we made our benchmarking visit to the University of Illinois.

But we have not merely waited for others to come to us to discover the benefits of our chemistry/math computer lab; we have developed an outreach program to share our success with other educators. As part of our networking efforts, we currently set aside three individual computer systems similar to what we have in the laboratory and loan them to high schools on a temporary basis. The software is quite versatile. While it challenges college level students, parts of it can also be used in high schools. We let individual high schools borrow one of the systems for a week, a month, or whatever amount of time fits their schedule. They borrow the PC, and the chemistry software is already installed on its hard drive. Last year, we loaned systems to several St. Joseph schools and other local schools through our outreach program. This past summer, we taught a course called "Special Topics in Chemistry" to a group of high school teachers from Missouri, Iowa, and Nebraska, to introduce them to the software and generate ideas on the pedagogy involved in teaching effectively with it. Most of the teachers in the class hope to install computer labs in their schools in the future. For now, some of them want to borrow our machines, so we will be taking outreach systems to their schools later this year.

A FINAL NOTE

We are very proud of what we have accomplished here at Northwest with our efforts to improve the quality of the laboratory learning experience. The fact that we researched, benchmarked, and planned for several years while trying to gather funding for the computer lab project worked to our advantage in the long run. Because we did not jump at the first option that presented itself, we were able to get a better, more efficient, and more flexible system. We know this is only the beginning, however. Adapting teaching methods and styles to accommodate and fully utilize the computer lab will take time. And, while our chemistry lab represents the finest educational technology available today, our entire chemistry program must also develop and evolve if it is to keep pace and earn us continuing accreditation from the American Chemical Society. We remain hopeful that, with the evident success of our chemistry/math computer lab, we may secure continuing support from students, faculty, university administrators, and the community to ensure that Northwest Missouri State University's chemistry program remains strong well into the twenty-first century.

HARLAN HIGGINBOTHAM

Harlan Higginbotham has taught chemistry at Northwest Missouri State University for thirty years. Along with Edward Farquhar — now the chair of the department — and other faculty, Higginbotham worked to develop the chemistry program at Northwest in order to earn the department ACS accreditation in 1970. He has a bachelor of science degree in Chemistry, Math, and Physics from Northwest, and a doctorate in Physical and Analytical Chemistry from Iowa State University.

ORDER FORM

Name_____

Mailing Address _____

City _____ State _____ Zip _____

____ The Culture for Quality: Effective Faculty Teams $24.95

____ CQI 1995: Making the Transition To Education $22.95

____ TQM: Implications in Higher Education $29.95

____ Quality Teaching $19.99

       Missouri residents add 6.725 % sales tax.

Make check or money order payable to
Prescott Publishing and mail with this order form to:
      Prescott Publishing Co.
      106 S. Main
      Maryville, MO 64468

Please charge my   ___ MasterCard
               ___ Visa
               ___ American Express
               ___ Discover

Card #_____

Exp. Date_____

     All pre-paid orders will receive FREE SHIPPING.

To request a copy of the Prescott Publishing Quality Catalog, or to make an order, call toll-free 1-800-528-5197 between 8 a.m. and 5 p.m. cental/standard time.